MENTAL ILLNESS in PERSPECTIVE:

History and Schools of Thought

by

ROBERT A. CLARK, M.D.

 Pacific Grove, California

Distributed by:

THE BOXWOOD PRESS
183 Ocean View Blvd.
Pacific Grove, California 93950

Phone: 408—375-9110

Library of Congress Card
No. 73-88484

Standard Book Number: 910286-29-9

Printed in U.S.A.

Preface

This book grew out of a series of lectures given at Eastern Pennsylvania Psychiatric Institute to the psychiatric residents over the past 10 or 12 years, chiefly under the direction of Dr. Alexandra Lubizka. The incentive to put them on paper came from an invitation to repeat the lectures at Friends Hospital under the auspices of the Department of Staff Development of the Northeast Community Mental Health Center of Philadelphia. I am grateful to Dr. Fred Honigman and to Dr. Gaston G. Trigos for their encouragement in the project. My secretary, Mrs. Marie Rinehart, spent many hours typing the first draft, the corrected draft, and the final draft. I owe much to her patient accuracy.

In my writing I consulted some original sources, but mostly, in the midst of the busy practice and the teaching of psychiatry, I have relied on the work of others. First there were standard works such as Zilboorg's *History of Medical Psychology.* Then came the contributions of specialists in the history of psychiatry: George Mora, George Rosen, Ilza Veith, and others. In the later chapters, especially on schools of psychiatric thought I owe a great debt to Dr. Henri Ellenberger. I first met him on a bridge at Rheinau in 1954 when the Swiss Society for Psychiatry and Neurology was meeting there. His chapter in *Existence,* edited by Rollo May, and his monumental book, *The Discovery of the Unconscious,* are mines of material and models of exposition.

I hope that this book will be of some value to young psychiatrists who are reviewing for their American Board exams, as well as to other students and practitioners who are looking for a brief survey of the field. May it encourage them to seek further.

Robert A. Clark, M.D.

8301 Forest Avenue
Elkins Park, Pa. 19117

Contents

Introduction

When we study the history of mental illness and attitudes toward it throughout the centuries, we can ask ourselves several questions. The first is, why, as practitioners of the mental health sciences, should we study their history at all? Psychiatry is a learned profession, allied to academic science on the one hand and to medicine on the other. It is not just a trade or technology. It has a reservoir of knowledge, theories and techniques still accumulating after nearly 200 years. "He who does not know history is condemned to repeat the mistakes of his ancestors," the saying goes. The member of a profession should know how the knowledge he uses has grown. He needs to know the problems his profession has faced, the theories about them, the methods of coping with them, their successes and their failures.

Our next question is: How can we best study the history of mental illness? Many historians used to be antiquarians—concerned with outmoded practices (and their quaint practitioners), contrasting them with modern methods, seldom attempting to understand the past or to relate it to the present. Other ways of studying history have since emerged (1). First was the writing of biographies of pioneers, reformers, and founders of schools—the "pantheon" approach. Then came optimistic demonstration of progress, ethical or scientific. More sophistication in recent years has led scholars back to the study of primary sources, including the writings of the pioneers and the records of their institutions. Recurrent themes in the history of ideas have been uncovered. Psychiatric thought and practices of each age are related to contemporary philosophy, economics, and sociology. I have made use of all these approaches. The ideal history, to my mind, should make appropriate use of whatever method is most illuminating.

Progress in the understanding and treatment of mental illness, compared to that in other disorders, has been both slow and uneven. The brain is the most complex thing we know of in the universe. It is not surprising, therefore, that medicine has made more progress, for instance, with the heart, which is only a delicate kind of pump. Only in recent years have we realized how closely attitudes toward mental illness are related to philosophical outlook and sociological structure. There is more cultural lag in our field than in most. For example, many people still believe in witchcraft, even educated men and women. Earlier attitudes toward mental illness persist in all of us, if not consciously, at least unconsiously. One reason for this persistence is that mental illness is more frightening than physical illness, and consequently harder to be objective about. In the presence of mental illness, therefore, unconscious feelings about it may

1

come to the surface and influence our thinking and actions, not only in our patients and their relatives and neighbors, but in ourselves.

The student of mental illness will find three threads woven into the fabric of its history. First is the red thread of fear and superstition, encouraging ignorance, neglect, and cruelty. Then are the two golden threads of humanity and science. Where humanitarianism practises alone there is danger of treating patients like helpless children. Science alone, untempered by humanity, may result in dehumanization. Patients become merely objects for statistics and experimentation. When science and humanity work together, each patient becomes a unique individual capable or potentially capable of becoming a responsible adult, and with the right to participate (or not) in scientific studies or in his treatment.

Chapter 1

ANCIENT TIMES

A. Egypt.

Already in ancient Egypt descriptions resembling present-day psychiatric illness have been found. Among the many papyruses discovered by archeologists, two refer to a condition very like hysteria (2). The Kahun Papyrus, from about 1900 B.C., describes a morbid state due to a displacement or "starvation" of the uterus. One case is that of "a woman who loves bed, she does not rise," another "pained in her teeth and jaws, she knows not how to open her mouth;" a third, "aching in all her limbs, with pain in the sockets of her eyes." Treatment was intended to drive the uterus back or to lure it to its proper place. Evil-tasting or foul-smelling substances were swallowed or inhaled to repel it, precious and sweet-smelling substances were applied to attract it. The Ebers Papyrus, from the 16th century B.C., gives a prescription of ship's tar and the dregs of beer to induce uterine descent, while sitting on a roll of cloth moistened with an infusion of pine sawdust to attract the uterus downward. A final measure was to place beneath the patient a wax ibis in charcoal—a magical substance invoking a god. The ibis was the Symbol of Toth—the god of wisdom, author of books on medicine, and the physician to the gods.

B. Classical Greece and Rome.

Our Western culture has two chief roots: the heritage of classical Greece and Rome on the one hand and the Judaeo-Christian tradition on the other. Of the two principal classical sources, the literary and the medical, the literary is the older. Among the earliest classical descriptions of mental illness are those in the works of the Greek tragedians: Sophocles, Aeschylus, and Euripedes.

1. Athenian Tragic Drama. In Athens during the fifth century B.C., each month had its festival. In Springtime was that of Dionysus, often called Bacchus. We think of him as the god of wine, but he was much more (3). He was the sap rising in the tree, the bringer of blossoms and fruits, the abundance of life, the blood pounding in the young animal. His ceremonies were more than revels. They were a particular kind of religious experience. Each year at the festival of Dionysus (4), tragedies were solemnly performed in the theater of the god. Like many other Greek festivals, each performance was a competition. Three poets were selected to present their dramas. At the end of the festival five judges awarded the prizes. The Athenian audiences were the most sophisticated of ancient times. Whatever the dramas portrayed had to appeal to the critical taste of both audience and judges.

(a) *Ajax:* The earliest play containing an account of mental illness is Sophocles' *Ajax.* Sophocles lived from 496 to 406 B.C. He was a sponsor for the introduction into Athens of the worship of Aesculapius, god of healing. *Ajax* is the earliest of his surviving plays, from about 460 B.C. During the seige of Troy, Athena, patron goddess of Athens, told Odysseus how Ajax was "crazed with jealousy for the armor of Achilles, which was given to you." (5). Ajax crept into the camp before Troy at night, intending to kill Odysseus and his men. Athena thus describes how she thwarted him; by

"... darkening his vision
with a veil of fantasy, which overpowered him
So that he turned his wrath upon the cattle,
The sheep, and all the unassorted spoil
That the drovers had in charge. On this horned host
He dealt his death-blows, hacking and slaughtering
To right and left; to his deluded fancy
Now it was the sons of Atreus he was mauling
And butchering .. I was there
To goad and drive him deeper into the pit
Of black delusion; till at last he paused,
And taking the beasts for human prisoners,
Roped up the cattle ... and marched them to his tent,
Where he is now tormenting them, like captives
Bound to the stake,
And now you too shall see
With your own eyes this hideous spectacle. ...
Stay, do not be afraid.
He shall not harm you; I will keep his eyes
Averted from your face."

Ajax appears from his tent, convinced he is holding Odysseus captive. Athena does not contradict him and allows him to return to his tent. She then turns to Odysseus and says:

"Therefore beware of uttering blasphemy
against the gods, beware of pride, puffed
By strength or substance."

In the next scene Ajax's consort, Tecmessa, reports that his mind has cleared:

"He understands; but now there is other pain
That he must bear, the bitter torment
Of seeing his own hand's mischief
The guilt that none can share."
He "... slowly, painfully, regained his senses
... uttered a loud cry
And beat his brow, and tumbling to the ground
... sat there with clutching fingers
Gripping his hair—sat for a long time silent...
He broke into such piteous cries of anguish...
And so he sits, utterly dejected;
Will take no food nor drink, but only sits."

The chorus tries to comfort him:

"Do not torment yourself for what is past.
What's done cannot be undone."

Tecmessa asks him not to throw himself suicidally into battle:

"O Ajax, have you the heart to leave your father
To face old age without you? Have you the heart
To leave your mother a long legacy
Of lonely years? ... Think of your son...
Can you do such a thing to him, and me?...
Have you forgotten me?"

Despite these words, Ajax plants his sword by the hilt in the ground,
while calling upon those avenging demons, the Furies:

"May...
The stern unresting Furies, see this death
And know that the sons of Atreus brought it on me:
And wipe them utterly out with deaths as vile
As their vile selves. Go to it, you swift avengers,
Drink deep, and spare not one of all their people!"

He kills himself. Odysseus convinces Agamemnon, the commander, that,
despite Ajax's disloyalty, madness and suicide, he should be buried as a
hero.

    This play describes two phases of functional mental illness—an acute
attack with delusions, hallucinations, and psychotic behavior, and second,
depression and suicide. The causes are immediate: jealousy, pride, and
the action of a goddess resulting in the acute psychosis, shame and despair
bringing on depression. There is no amnesia for the psychosis and there is
insight into the nature of the illness right afterward. The same pride caus-

ing Ajax's jealousy of Odysseus brings about his shame. To become ill
requires divine intervention; recovery is spontaneous. An attempt at psychotherapy appeals to the hero's love of his consort, his son, and his parents.
But his pride is too strong. Calling vengeance on his enemies, he turns his
anger against himself and dies. The attitudes of those about him contain
fear of the evil effect of his glance, compassion and a desire to help, and
forgiveness for his actions and for his foolish pride. The need for constant
watch over a depressed man is clearly recognized.

(b) Orestes: The second play is by Aeschylus: *The Libation Bearers,*
the middle play of a triology concerned with Orestes, produced in 458 B.C.
(6). Orestes returns from the Trojan War to discover that his father,
Agamemnon, has been killed by his mother and her paramour. In revenge
he kills her, at the bidding of the god Apollo. According to the old Pelasgian faith, prevailing before the Hellenes came from the north, anyone who
kills a blood relative must be punished, no matter what the reason for the
killing. After his deed, Orestes has a terrifying vision of the Furies—female
emissaries of vengeance. He cries out to the Chorus, who are witnesses to
the scene:

> "Look, women, see them there! Like Gorgons, with grey cloaks,
> And snakes swarming round their bodies!
> ... To me these living horrors are not imaginary;
> I know them—avenging hounds incensed by a
> mother's blood."

The chorus tries to reassure him, saying:

> "That blood is still a fresh pollution on your hands,
> Therefore your mind's distracted. What more natural?"

But Orestes is not so easily relieved:

> "... More and more of them, Look there!
> And see—their dreadful eyes dripping with bloody pus!"

The Chorus, seeing he needs more than they can do, says:

> "Go quickly then where cleansing waits for you: stretch out
> Your hand to Apollo, and he will free you from this torment."

Orestes replies: "I know you do not see these things; but I see them. I am
lashed and driven! I can't bear it, I must escape."

The final play of the trilogy, *The Eumenides,* first discloses Orestes at the Apollo's shrine, recovered. Apollo orders the Furies from his temple.

The next scene takes the audience to the temple of Athena at Athens. Athena herself presides at Orestes' trial—the first forensic psychiatry case in the history of drama. She asks the Furies (the chorus in this play): "where can such a fugitive find rest and peace?" Orestes testifies, speaking sanely in his own behalf, admitting guilt, but justifying his act. The jury of twelve Athenians votes a tie. Athena casts the acquitting vote.

> "No mother gave me birth. Therefore the father's claim
> Of male supremacy in all things, save to give
> Myself in marriage, wins my whole heart's loyalty.
> Therefore a woman's death, who killed her husband, is
> I judge, outweighed in grievousness by his."

The high gods of the newer Hellene faith thus win out over the more primitive doctrine of vengeance of the old Pelasgian religion. "The old is trampled by the new."

Ajax had called on the Furies to avenge him. Orestes has vengeance wreaked upon by these same primitive spirits. He hallucinates them, responding with horror. Attempts at reassurance failing, the chorus advises him to cleanse himself of his pollution by appealing to Apollo. Having done this, he recovers at Apollo's shrine. He retains his sanity during the trial. In the name of the Hellenic gods, Orestes is forgiven for his matricide.

(c) Heracles: The last of the great Athenian tragedians is Euripedes. The theme of madness often comes up in his melodramatic, yet profound dramas. *Heracles* (7), written about 420 B.C., resembles the Orestian plays. Heracles, after completing his labors, remains in Hades for a time. While he is gone his father's throne at Thebes is usurped by Lyseus. Heracles' wife and three sons are threatened with death. The hero returns in time to rescue them. Suddenly the figure of Madness appears. In *The Eumenides* the Furies invoke their mother, Night. In *Heracles,* Madness is called "unmarried child of blackest Night." He is sent by Hera to invlict vengeance on Heracles for Zeus' infidelity to her with Heracles' mother. Reluctantly he carries out Hera's order, saying:

> "He shall kill his sons and, killing, shall not know
> He kills what he begot, until my madness leaves him."

He describes Heracles in a frenzy:

> "Look: already, head writhing, he leaps the starting-post;
> Jumps and now stops; his eyeballs bulge, and pupils roll;

His breath comes heaving up, a bull about to charge!
And now he bellows up the horrid fates from hell;
He groans and shouts; he dances to the pipes of terror!"
" ... and froth began to trickle down his bearded chin
... laughing like a maniac."

Deluded that he is pursuing Erystheus (for whom he performed his celebrated labors) and killing Erystheus' children, he kills his own sons. He sends an arrow through his wife as she tries to protect the last of them. Athena stops him as he is about to kill his father. Tied down, he falls into exhausted sleep. Sympathy and horror are both expressed: "I do not know one man alive more miserable than this." Heracles' normal self is set apart from his madness: they are "murdered by your madness," rather than killed by Heracles himself. His father fears that "he will destroy us all: father, city and his house." Yet when he rouses he says: "How strangely my muddled senses swim as on a choppy sea ... I am bewildered." He asks for help and explanations. His father approaches him, despite his fear, asking: "Tell me if you are sane?" Heracles replies: "I cannot remember being mad." The father gently shows him what he has done. Heracles is overwhelmed by grief and self-blame. "Let me hurl myself down from sheer rock ... As expunge with fire this body's madness and burn away this guilt." He covers his head to shelter others from harm and pollution.

At this point Theseus, legendary king of Athens, enters and says: "I come to share his grief." He speaks to Heracles: "Lift up your head and show your face to friends ... What do I care if your misfortunes fall on me? ... you saved me from the dead ... This is courage in a man: to bear unflinchingly what heaven sends." When Heracles cries: "Away, rash friend, flee my foul pollution," Theseus replies: "Where there is love, contagion cannot come." Heracles, reassured, renounces Zeus, his reputed father, and Hera, Zeus' wife and his tormentor, accepting Amphytrion as his father. Theseus adds: ... "be patient, suffer what you must, and do not yield to grief. Fate exempts no man; all men are flawed, and so the gods, unless the poets lie." He offers Heracles a home and a share of his wealth in Athens: "For now you need a friend." Heracles refuses to believe that divinities can commit crimes: "If a god is truly god, he is perfect," but accepts Theseus' offer.

In Heracles we see madness striking just when least expected, at a moment of triumph. *Madness,* like the Furies, a child of Night (perhaps because night is a time of fear, ruled by the moon) attacks at the bidding of jealous Hera, even though Heracles cannot be justly blamed for his parents' transgression. Here we have a vision of a frenzy—analogous to our modern acute schizophrenia, catatonic excitement or post-epileptic furor. Since he recovers so quickly, an acute delirium with clouding of consciousness and delusionary fantasies is suggested, rather than schizophrenia. Like Ajax,

Heracles is overwhelmed with grief, but unlike him, he is persuaded to live by the man whose life he once saved and who does not fear the contagion of pollution. Heracles, a demigod, resigns from his divine role and accepts his humanity. With Theseus as counselor and friend, he begins his grief work, restored to the human race, his faith in the gods unchanged.

(d) The Bacchae: Euripedes has more to say about madness in *The Bacchae,* his last and (some think) his greatest play, from about 407 B.C. (8). Its theme concerns Dionysus himself, the "spirit of revel and rapture." Pentheus, the young king of Thebes, denies the divinity of Dionysus. The seer Theresias says to Pentheus, "you were out of your mind before: now you are raving mad." Pentheus had ordered his men to destroy Theresias' shrine and to arrest the effeminate stranger from Phrygia, Dionysus in disguise. Pentheus, literal-minded conservative, suppresses novel religious observances by force. Challenged by Dionysus' power, his mind begins to crack, unable to assimilate so different a conception of life. For Dionysus

> " ... delights in banquets;
> And his dear love is Peace, giver of wealth,
> Savior of young men's lives—a goddess rare!
> In wine, his gift that charms all griefs away,
> Alike both rich and poor may have their part.
> His enemy is the man who has no care
> To pass his years in happiness and health,
> His days in quiet and his nights in joy,
> Watchful to keep aloof both mind and heart
> From men whose pride claims more than mortals may."

When Dionysus appears, he describes how he has driven his dead mother's Theban sisters "frantic out of doors" to the mountains. Indeed "the whole female population ... I drove raving from their homes," for "Thebes must learn ... that my Bacchic revels are something beyond her present knowledge." His inspiration is much more than that of drunkenness. It contains power to fortell the future as well.

When Pentheus spoke of binding Dionysus, the god said: "I am sane, you are mad." When Pentheus went ahead regardless, Dionysus showed his power: "I made a mockery of him. He thought he was binding me; but he fed himself on delusion—he neither took hold of me nor even touched me. Near the stall where he took me ... he found a bull; and he was tying his rope around the bull's knees and horns, panting with rage, dripping sweat, and biting his lips." Then he snatched up his sword and stabbed at a phantom figure of Dionysus that the god had conjured up.

As Dionysus calms Pentheus, a herdsman comes to tell about the Bacchae in the mountains. He emphasizes at first their seemliness and lack of sexual license. When dancing and calling upon Dionysus, they attack the cattle pastured there: "tearing our cows limb from limb ... and bulls ... dragged down by the soft hands of girls. They stripped the flesh off their bodies faster than you could wink your royal eyes ... They carried fire on their heads, and their hair was not burnt." He advises the king to receive the god into their city.

Dionysus invites the king to go with him to the mountain to see for himself. As though entranced, the king allows himself to be dressed as a woman (so that he will not be harmed), though expressing shame and fear of being laughed at. When they come upon where the Bacchae are, Dionysus betrays Pentheus to them: "I bring you the man who made a mockery of you, and of me, and of my holy rites. Now punish him." They (including his mother) pull Pentheus out of a tree, and tear him in pieces as they did the cattle. His mother, Agave, "was foaming at the mouth, her eyes were rolling wildly. She was not in her right mind; she was under the power of Dionysus." Thinking it is a lion's head, she takes his head to her father, Cadmus, as though it were a trophy of the hunt. As he talks gently to her, she says: "I feel a change in my mind; my thoughts are somehow clearer." He asks her whose head is it she holds in her arms. "A lion's," she replies. When he asks her to look straight at it, she cries out: "O gods, what horror! ... It is Pentheus' head I hold in my accursed hand." He informs her that she killed him, adding "your guilt is not greater than his." He ends: "If there be any man who derides the unseen word, let him consider the death of Pentheus, and acknowledge the gods!" She expresses her grief and disposes her son's limbs for burial in accordance with established ritual. Dionysus sends her into exile.

This profound and moving play describes three kinds of madness. The first is that of the youthful king, Pentheus. Swayed by the arrogance of unaccustomed power, he tries to crush by force deep religious feelings which he cannot allow himself to experience. The seer, Theresias, recognizes this arrogance as a kind of madness, which prepares the soil for the frenzied acts of Pentheus when he sees his narrow beliefs threatened.

The second kind of madness is not that of the rigid and threatened ego, but rather an overwhelming impulsive rush of feeling from the psychic depths, induced by Dionysus himself. Dionysus clouded Pentheus' mind, much as Athena bemused Ajax. He can also call out the transcendent frenzy of the Dionysiac possession, shown by the Theban women. It is primitive but asexual. It endows them with superhuman strength as they unite themselves with brute creation like carnivorous beasts. Later Pentheus' mother, Agave, is portrayed somewhat as Heracles had been in the previous play—unaware of the identity of her son, not even knowing he was human—

In a passage showing Euripedes' knowledge of the influence of a calm counselor and parent on an acutely disturbed person, Agave returns to sane reality, painful though it must be. Her grief work is helped by the burial ritual as well as by her father's words and manner.

2. Herodotus: The first master of Greek prose was Herodotus, the historian. In the course of his lengthy history of the Persian wars, written in the 5th century B.C. (about the time of the plays we have been quoting), he describes instances of mental illness.

He tells of the irreverent behavior of Cambyses, king of Persia. While in Egypt, Cambyses broke open ancient tombs, and jeered at the statue of a god, and even burned sacred images. "In view of all this," wrote Herodotus, "I have no doubt whatever that Cambyses was completely out of his mind; it is the only possible explanation of his ... mockery of everything which ancient law and custom have made sacred in Egypt ... Everyone ... believes his own native customs, and the religion he was brought up in, to be the best ... it is unlikely that anyone but a madman would mock at such things."

A more striking example, not only of irreverence, but of extraordinary behavior, is Herodotus' story of Cleomenes, king of Sparta. "He had always been a little queer ... but no sooner had he returned to Sparta than he lost his wits completely, and began poking his staff into the face of everyone he met ... His relatives put him in the stocks. As he was lying there ... he noticed that all his guards had left him except one." He induced this man to give him a knife, with which he "began to mutilate himself, beginning on his shins. He sliced his flesh into strips, working upwards ... until he reached his belly ... This finished him, and most people in Greece think that his unpleasant death was due to the fact that he corrupted the Priestess at Delphi ... the Athenians, however, put it down to his destruction of the sacred precinct of Demeter and Persephone," at Eleusis; "while the Argives maintained that it was a punishment for the acts of treachery and and sacrilege he committed when ... he fetched the Argive fugitives from the temple ... and cut them to pieces, and then showed such contempt for the grave itself where the temple stood that he burned it down." On another page Herodotus gives an explanation with a more modern ring: "His own countrymen, however, deny that his madness was a punishment from heaven, they are convinced ... that he lost his wits because, in his association with the Scythians, he had acquired the habit of drinking his wine neat!"

3. Plato: For a theoretical formulation of what dramatists and historians wrote about intuitively, we must wait for Plato, in the next century. In his dialogue, the *Phaedrus*, he has Socrates say: (10) "... madness was of two kinds, the one produced by human disease, the other by an inspired departure from established usages ... And the inspired we divide into four parts, and distributing them among four heavenly powers, we set down the madness of prophecy to the inspiration of Apollo; of mysteries, to the inspiration of Dionysus; to the Muses again we ascribe the madness of poesy; and the fourth, to Aphrodite and Eros."

In the same dialogue, on the subject of inspirational madness, he said: "... we owe our greatest blessings to madness, if only it be granted by Heaven's bounty. For the prophetess at Delphi ... and the priestesses of Dodona, have in their moments of madness done great and glorious service to the men and the cities of Greece ... As much then as divination is a more perfect, and a more precious thing than augury (practised by people not out of their senses, by observing birds and other signs) ... so much more glorious is madness than sober sense, the inspiration of Heaven than the creation of men. Again, for those sore plagues and dire afflictions which ... lingered in certain families as the wraith of some old ancestral guilt, madness devised a remedy ... for it fled for refuge to prayer and services of the gods ... it made the sufferer whole ... by showing him the way of escape from the evils that encompassed him, if only he were rightly frenzied and possessed. And thirdly, there is a possession and a madness inspired by the Muses, which seizes upon a tender and a virgin soul, and, stirring it up to rapturous frenzy, adorns in ode and other verse the countless deeds of elder time for the instruction of after ages ... The poetry of sense fades into obscurity before the poetry of madness." Last was "the madness of love ... the best of all."

E. R. Dodds, the British classical scholar, has a chapter in his book, *The Greeks and the Irrational,* (11) on *The Blessings of Madness.* He notes that years before Plato, Herodotus had distinguished between ordinary and divine madnesses. Madness could result from heavy drinking (as Herodotus realized) or could accompany epilepsy. When the body is seriously deranged it is not surprising that the mind should be affected also.

Dodds noted that on the one hand the mentally afflicted were shunned because subject to a divine curse and therefore dangerous, and on the other hand regarded with awe, for they were in contact with the supernatural world. "The dividing line between common insanity and prophetic madness is in fact hard to draw."

4. **Medical Sources:** Medicine among the ancient Greeks and Romans had its origins in the worship of the god Asklepios, called Aesculapius in Latin. In Greece the center of his worship was at Epidauros. His cult was not introduced into Athens until the 4th century, B.C. Sophocles, as I have said, was one of its sponsors. It came to Rome in the last decade of the 3rd century after an outbreak of plague. In that century a great center for religious healing was at Pergamum in Asia Minor. I had the impressive experience in 1966 of walking among the ruins of the Aesculapian

temple there.

The sick man or woman who came to an Aesculapian temple was expected to sleep overnight in a circular underground chamber under which a stream flowed. In Pergamum in 1966 this spring was still flowing after more than 2000 years. Whether or not the god would heal the sick man depended upon the vision or the dream he had that night. If the god or either of his totem animals, the dog or the snake, appeared to him, he would be cured.

(a) *Hippocrates.* The earliest Greek physician whose work we know is Hippocrates. He was born on the island of Kos, in the 5th century, B.C. in the Eastern Aegean Sea, where the ruins of an Aesculapian temple still are. He went to Athens, where he was a contemporary of Sophocles, Pericles and many others whose names we know so well. Many of his writings and those of his disciples have been preserved. In them are descriptions of illnesses much like ones we now see, including mania, melancholia and paranoia. Like the Egyptians, he attributed symptoms we would now call psychoneurotic to the wanderings of the uterus. Respecting epilepsy, we read that it was "in no way more divine nor sacred than other diseases, but has a natural cause ... It is not a god which injures the body, but disease." Elsewhere we find: "all (diseases) are divine and all human." (12).

If I may return to Plato for a moment, the most graphic description of hysteria by a Greek comes from his dialogue, the Timaeus: "The womb is an animal which longs to generate children. When it remains barren too long after puberty, it is distressed ... and straying about in the body ... it impedes respiration and brings the sufferer into the extremist anguish and provokes all manner of diseases." Such disturbances continued until the womb was "appeased by passion and love." We observe little progress here since the Egyptians 1300 years before, but we must remember that Hippocrates and Plato were men—not women.

(b) *Galen.* By the 2nd century A.D., matters had improved. The Greek physician whose writings have come down to us most complete is Galen. Born in Pergamum, he practiced in Rome. He described a woman in love with a dancer who was depressed and "suffering from ... either a melancholy dependent on black bile or else something she was unwilling to confess." (13). Other physicians, he said, "have no clear conception of how the body tends to be affected by mental conditions. Possibly also they do not know that the pulse is altered by quarrels and alarms." Galen rejected the idea that in hysteria the uterus wanders in the body like an animal, yet he thought hysteria to be due to a local "engorgement" of the uterus.

(c) Soranus. Galen's contemporary, Soranus, was born in Ephesus. He described mania as "an impairment of the reason resulting from a bodily disease or indisposition," often arising from observable causes, such as ... drunkenness, sleeplessness, excesses of venery, anger, grief ... superstitious fear ... straining of the mind in study or business ... the drinking of drugs ... and finally, the suppression of the menses in women." "Mania ... manifests itself now in anger, now in merriment, now in futility, now ... in an overpowering fear of things which are quite harmless." It is sometimes continuous and at other times relieved by intervals of remission. "The name melancholia," he wrote, "comes from vomiting black bile, but the notion that black bile causes the disease is false." "The signs of melancholy ... are ... mental anguish and distress, dejection, silence, animosity toward members of the household ... sometimes a longing for death."

Schools of medicine existed in Soranus' time as they do now. His ways of treatment were those of the "methodists," and were characterized by moderation and humanity. He advised against putting patients in dark rooms, giving them starvation diets, putting them in bonds, giving them drugs in excess, bleeding them from both arms, or flogging them. Instead he recommended having "the patient lie in a moderately light room, perfectly quiet ... on the ground floor, for victims ... have often jumped out of windows ... Instruct the servants to correct the patient's aberrations while giving them a sympathetic hearing." He suggested "passive exercise, walking, vocal exercise and reading that is easy to understand ... If he is unacquainted with literature, give him problems if he is a farmer, problems in navigation if he is a pilot." He advised caution with music, for "in some cases music arouses men to madness," and with love, for "in many cases love is the very cause of madness." (14)

Summary. In the classical age we see fear of the mentally ill—when Athena tells Odysseus not to be afraid; that she will keep Ajax's eyes averted, or when patients are starved and flogged. We also see evidence of humanity—the recognition of suffering, help by physicians, laymen, heroes and divinities, humane medical care. We see the beginnings of scientific observation, description, classification and understanding. Fear was strong, but nevertheless compassion was felt, knowledge was accumulating, and understanding had begun.

BIBLIOGRAPHY

1. Benjamin Nelson, in: *Psychiatry and Its Histories*, edited by George Mora and J. L. Brand, Thomas, Springfield, Ill., 1970, pp 229-259.

2. Ilza Veith, *Hysteria, the History of a Disease*, U. of Chicago Press, Chicago 1965, p 2 ff.

3. E. R. Dodds, *Euripedes' Bacchae*, Introduction, Oxford U. Press, 1944

4. Gilbert Murray, *Euripedes and His Age*, Home University Library, New York, 1913.

5. *Sophocles, Electra and Other Plays*, translated by E. F. Wathing, Penguin Books, Baltimore, undated.

6. *Aeschylus, The Oresteian Trilogy*, translated by Philip Vellacott, Penguin Books, Baltimore, undated.

7. *The Complete Greek Tragedies*, vol. III *Heracles*, translated by William Arrowsmith, U. of Chicago Press, Chicago, 1959.

8. *The Complete Greek Tragedies*, vol. III, *The Bacchae*, translated by Rex Warner, U. of Chicago Press, Chicago, 1959.

9. *Herodotus, The Histories*, Penguin Books, Baltimore, 1954, pp. 190 ff and 386 ff.

10. *Plato, Phaedrus*, Everyman's Library, E. P. Dutton, N. Y., 1910.

11. E. R. Dodds, *The Greeks and the Irrational*, Beacon Press, Boston, 1957.

12. *The Genuine Works of Hippocrates*, translated by Francis Adams (1849), William and Wilkins, Baltimore, 1946.

13. S. W. Jackson, *Galen on Mental Disorders*, J. Behav. Sci., 5:365, 1969.

14. *Documentary History of Psychiatry*, Charles E. Goshen, Philosophical Library, New York, 1967, pp. 18-33.

Chapter 2

THE JUDAEO-CHRISTIAN TRADITION

Introduction. The second most important Western source of ideas and attitudes concerning mental illness is the Judaeo-Christian, embodied in the Bible and in Jewish and Christian history. What makes their Scriptures so important is not only their historical value as ancient records, but also the fact that for millions of Jews and Christians throughout the world, even at the present day, they are holy writ. Every word is taken to be inspired by God and therefore literally true. Many of our patients (and their relatives) will believe them word for word. Even most people who think they are no longer believers were brought up in this tradition by parents or grandparents who *did* believe. Consequently belief in the ideas and attitudes of the Bible is a short distance beneath the surface of consciousness in nearly all of us.

1. The Bible. The Biblical tradition is not always clear. Many Jews and Christians do not know the Bible well. They have forgotten what they were taught, or they were told only certain favorite stories and passages, by clergymen and teachers who made their own selections and interpretations. Fear and superstition have clouded the Biblical tradition, causing believers to think and act contrary to its humane portions.

What does the Bible say about mental illness? Three well-known examples come to mind: Saul and Nebuchadnezzar from the Old Testament, and the man possessed by evil spirits in the New Testament.

A. The Old Testament. In the first book of Samuel, King Saul is denounced by the prophet for having sinned. He had not killed all the cattle and sheep belonging to the Amelakites, a nation just defeated. At the Lord's direction the prophet Samuel anointed David (without the king's knowledge) as Saul's successor. Soon after (1):

"... the Spirit of the Lord departed from Saul and an evil spirit from the Lord troubled him."Recognizing his condition, Saul's servants said to him: "Let our Lord now command thy servants ... to seek out a man who is a cunning player on an harp: and it shall come to pass, when the evil spirit from God is upon thee, that he shall play with his hand, and thou shalt be well." One of the servants volunteered: "I have seen a son of Jesse ... that is cunning in playing, and a mighty valiant man, and prudent in matters, and a comely person, and the Lord is with him."Saul sent messengers to Jesse to summon David. "And David came to Saul and stood before him, and he loved him greatly and he became his armorbearer ... When the evil spirit from God was upon Saul ... David took an harp, and played with his hand: so Saul was refreshed, and was well, and the evil spirit departed from him."

The following chapter tells how David killed Goliath, the Philistine champion. The Philistines were routed and many were slaughtered. During subsequent rejoicing, the Jewish women said to each other: "Saul has slain his thousands, and David his ten thousands." Hearing this, Saul was very wroth ... and said, "... what can he have more but the kingdom." The story continues: "And it came to pass on the morrow, that the evil spirit from God came upon Saul, and he prophesied in the midst of the house: and David played ... as at other times." This time the music did not calm Saul. Instead the king cast a javelin at David, "and David avoided out of his presence ... And Saul was afraid of David, because the Lord was with him, and was departed from Saul."

The story concerning Nebuchadnezzar, king of Babylon, in the book of Daniel (2) appears to be a description of mental illness. Nebuchadnezzar, the antagonist of Daniel, the prophet, boasts: "Is not this great Babylon, that I have built for the house of the kingdom of the might of my power, and for the honor of my majesty? ... While the word was in the king's mouth, there fell a voice from heaven, saying, O king Nebuchadnezzar, to thee it is spoken; thy kingdom is departed from thee ... And they shall drive thee from man and thy dwelling shall be with the beasts of the field: they shall make thee to eat grass as oxen, and seven times shall pass over thee until thou know that the most High ruleth in the kingdom of men, and give to whomsoever he will ... The same hour was the thing fulfilled upon Nebuchadnezzar, and he was driven from men, and did eat grass as oxen, and his body was wet with the dew of heaven, until his hairs were grown like eagle's feathers and his nails were as bird's claws ... And at the end of the days, I, Nebuchadnezzar, lifted up mine eyes unto heaven, and mine understanding returned unto me, and I blessed the most High ... And I was established in my kingdom and excellent majesty was added unto me."

These examples tell us several things about the understanding of mental illness among the Jews in ancient times. In both instances mental illness was caused by God. Being uncompromising monotheists, the Jews had no misgivings in saying that an evil spirit could emanate from God as well as a beneficent spirit. The evil spirit is called forth by sin. Saul disobeyed God's will and was jealous. Nebuchadnezzar harbored overweening pride and boastfulness. David's music, and Saul's love for him, persuaded God to withdraw the evil spirit. When Saul's love changed to jealousy, the evil spirit (and the illness) returned. Without Saul's love, the music did not work, and Saul's murderous act ensued. Nebuchadnezzar was condemned to behave like an animal. No longer human, he ate grass and his hair grew.

Not until the king acknowledged the power and authority of the universal God was his sanity restored and his kingdom returned.

B. *The New Testament.* The New Testament example was composed, most scholars agree, early in the second century of the Christian era, over 200 years after the book of Daniel was written, and more than 1000 years after the time of king Saul. This is how the story goes from the earliest gospel (3): "And [Jesus and his disciples] came over unto the side of the sea [of Gallilee], into the country of the Gadarenes ... And when [Jesus] was come out of the ship, immediately there met him out of the tombs a man with an unclean spirit ... who had his dwelling among the tombs: and no man could bind him, no, not with chains. Because that he had been often bound with fetters broken in pieces: neither could any man tame him ... And always, night and day, he was in the mountains, and in the tombs, crying, and cutting himself with stones ... But when he saw Jesus afar off, he ran and worshipped him ... And he cried with a loud voice, and said, *What have I to do with thee, Jesus, thou Son of the most high God. I adjure thee by God, that thou torment me not* ... For [Jesus] said unto him, *Come out of the man, thou unclean spirit* ... And he asked him, *What is thy name?* And he answered, saying, *My name is Legion; for we are many* ... Now there was nigh unto the mountains a great herd of swine feeding ... And all the devils besought him, saying, *Send us into the swine* ... and forthwith Jesus gave them leave. And the unclean spirits ... entered into the swine: and the herd ran violently down a steep place into the sea and were choked in the sea ... Him that was possessed with the devil and had the Legion [was] sitting and clothed, and in his right mind ... And when [Jesus] was come unto the ship, he that had been possessed with the devil prayed him that he might be with him ... Howbeit Jesus ... saith unto him, *Go home to thy friends, and tell them how great things the Lord had done for thee and had compassion on thee.*"

This passage informs us that either in Jesus' time, or at the time the gospel was written, madmen were banished to bare, rocky hills and bound with fetters. They were believed to have superhuman strength capable of breaking the chains. At the same time it was realized that they suffered, not sleeping, and cutting themselves in their anguish. They also had the power to recognize a prophet at once, contrary to the spiritual blindness of most sane men. In the 3rd chapter of Mark when some of Jesus' friends heard that many crowded around after he was said to have cured sickness, "they went out to lay hold on him, for they said, he is beside himself." The Gadarene story soon becomes confusing. It is not clear whether the afflicted man himself is speaking or whether the unclean spirits are speaking through him. In any case, Jesus finally, at the spirits' request, sends them into the bodies of swine—also unclean. The madman, like both Saul (in his first attack) and Nebuchadnezzar, recovers. The most significant phrase in the whole passage is the last, that Jesus *had compassion on* him—meaning, that he recognized the man's suffering and his continued humanity, despite his being possessed. Another point of difference between Old and New Testament times is that the demons are separate entities from God. They are devils, minions of Satan, the personification of evil. Belief is no longer so purely monotheistic as that which prevailed when the history of king Saul was written. That they are banished into swine suggests a link with the underworld deities of the Greeks. Swine were sacred to Demeter, goddess of the productive earth. When sacrificed, their blood was allowed to run down into the earth, rather than ascend into heaven with the smoke of a burnt sacrifice. Presumably the Gadarenes were not Jews. One hopes they got paid for their swine! The sharp division between the heavens and the earth—the realm of Yahweh on the one hand and that of pagan deities and of Satan on the other, may come partly from Greek and Roman mythology and partly from Zoroastrian doctrine by way of Persia. Zoroastrians taught that the God of light was eternally in conflict with the Spirit of darkness.

2. Witchcraft. During the Dark Ages we know very little about the condition or treatment of the mentally ill. The rite of exorcism was preserved in the rituals of the Roman Catholic Church well into modern times. Jesus' power to cast out "devils" was transmitted to his apostles, and thence to the priests of the apostolic church.

In the later years of the Roman Empire, superstition became rampant. A great many lead plates have been discovered, especially in Italy, carrying curses directed against enemies. Witchcraft and the fear of witches flourished throughout the Middle Ages and far into the Renaissance. Both the practice and the fear of witchcraft were founded upon good biblical authority.

A. The Old Testament. In the book of Exodus (22,18) occurs that famous (and infamous) verse: "Thou shalt not suffer a witch to live." In the Douay version, until recently the official Roman Catholic translation, the verse reads "wizard" instead of "witch," but the meaning was taken to be the same. Deuteronomy (18:10) is less severe: "There shall not be found among you ... an enchanter, or a witch ... or a wizard or a necromancer. For all that do these things are an abomination into the Lord: and because of these abominations the Lord thy God doth drive them out from before thee"—into exile.

These prohibitions did not prevent king Saul, after he drove David away, from consulting a necromancer (I. Samuel 28, 6-9):

"And when Saul enquired of the Lord, the Lord answered him not ... Then said Saul unto his servants, *Seek me a woman that hath a familiar spirit, that I may go to her, and inquire of her.* And his servants said to him, *Behold there is a woman ... at Endor.* And Saul disguised himself and came to the woman by night: and he said ... *Bring me up whom I shall name unto thee* ... And the woman said ... *thou knowest ... Saul ... hath cut off those that hath familiar spirits and the wizards out of the land, wherefore then layest thou a snare for my life to cause me to die?"* Saul persuaded her to proceed. The prophet Samuel appeared out of the earth. Samuel predicted that Saul and his sons would die. The next day, in battle with the Philistines, Saul and his sons were defeated and Saul killed himself.

B. The New Testament. In the New Testament, witchcraft is rarely mentioned. Here is one instance, from the letter of Paul to the Galatians (5:19-21): "Now the works of the flesh are manifest ... adultery, fornication ... idolatry, witchcraft ... heresies ... murders, drunkenness, revellings and such like ... they which do such things shall not inherit the kingdom of God." This is certainly a milder penalty, during this life, if not in the "next." The offense of witchcraft is nevertheless one of the worst.

From the 15th to the 18th centuries waves of superstitious fear and persecution swept through Europe and splashed over into the colonies in America. Records of the investigations, trials and executions give a vast amount of information regarding the prevalence and forms of psychiatric illness during these centuries. The men who made these records correctly observed that, although witchcraft was condemned in the Scriptures, it was assumed to exist. Its practitioners had great power and its victims were in great danger.

C. Malleus Malificarum: One of the best sources for the early years of witchcraft trials is the *Malleus Malificarum*, the Hammer of the Wicked. (4). This is a report of the investigations of two Dominican friars, Henry Kramer and James Sprenger, into witchcraft in North Germany, authorized by a bull of Pope Innocent the Eighth, dated 1484. A "best seller," their book was used as a text by inquisitors and judges throughout Europe and America for more than two centuries.

For the existence of witchcraft Kramer and Sprenger laid down three conditions: the devil, a witch, and the permission of God. A great majority of witches are women. They found three general vices in wicked woman: infidelity, ambition, and lust. Particularly given to witchcraft are "adulterous drabs and whores," who cast spells especially upon the act of generation. Wicked women infect the venereal act and conception by seven methods:

1. By inclining men to inordinate passion.
2. By obstructing their generative force.
3. By removing the members accommodated to that act.
4. By changing men into beasts by their magic art.
5. By destroying the generative force in women.
6. By procuring abortion.
7. By offering children to devils.

God permits witchcraft more in the case of the generative powers, because of their greater "corruption" than in the case of other human actions.

Anxious to carry out their mission carefully and responsibly, Kramer and Sprenger concerned themselves with the distinctions between natural phenomena and those due to witchcraft. When a member can in no way be stirred, this is frigidity of nature; when it is stirred and erect but cannot perform that is a sign of witchcraft. A bewitched man can be capable with other women, but not with the one (presumably his wife). Whether an illness be caused by witchcraft can be told in several ways. First, from the judgment of doctors: if an external cause is not an infection, it must be witchcraft. Second, incurability: if relieved by no drugs, but rather aggravated by them. Third, if of sudden onset.

The investigators were also interested in the behavior characteristic of witches. The witches themselves, they wrote, "have often been seen lying on their backs in the fields or the woods, naked up to the very navel, and it has been apparent from the disposition of those limbs and members which pertain to the venereal act ... as also from the agitation of their legs and thighs, that, invisibly to the bystanders, they have been copulating with Incubus devils." Incubus devils were evil spirits who made a practice of seducing women into the devil's service by sexual means. They ask: "what is to be thought of those witches who ... collect male organs in great numbers, as many as 20 or 30 members together, and put them in a bird's nest, or shut them up in a box, where they move among themselves like living members, and eat oats and corn, as has been seen by many, and is a matter of common report?" They quote one William of Paris: "At times women think they have been made pregnant by the Incubus, and their bellies grow to an enormous size; but when the time of parturition comes, their swelling is relieved by no more than the expulsion of a great quantity of wind." They note that "witches continue to sin after great punishments have been often inflicted upon many other witches," as though seeking for punishment, or at least unaffected by or indifferent to the experience of others.

These Christian fathers were convinced that the death penalty is justified, except perhaps for priests: "If a man be convicted, and refuse to be

converted and abjure his heresy, he must at once be burned, if he is a layman. For if they who counterfeit money are summarily put to death, how
much more must they who counterfeit the Faith?"

The cases which the fathers describe with vivid brevity, show us that
hysteria was rife in the 15th century. I have already mentioned the case
of pseudocyesis quoted from William of Paris. Men had symptoms un-
mistakably like those of hysteria. There was the man with an obstinate
wife. "When he struck her on the buttock, after she dared him to beat
her, he fell to the ground, lost his senses and was sick many days," perhaps frightened by his own temerity. There was the case of the possessed
priest. The devil made him thrust his tongue far out of his mouth whenever he passed by a church. He said: "I cannot help myself at all, for so
he uses my limbs and organs, my tongue and my lungs, whenever he
pleases, causing me to speak or to cry out ... and when I try to engage in
prayer he attacks me more violently, thrusting out my tongue." This
priest may have mistaken his vocation. Then there was the honest parish
priest of Basel, Switzerland, who was two centuries ahead of his time. He
"fondly held the opinion, or rather error, that there was no witchcraft
in the world, but that it only existed in the imagination of men who attributed such things to witches ... He felt himself bewitched below the
waist, so he always had to be supported by the arms of other men when
he wished to go to church; and so he remained for three years, under the
care of his mother."

D. The American Colonies: Two centuries later, across the Atlantic
Ocean and in a Protestant land, the practice of witchcraft was still going
on (5). At Hartford, Connecticut, in 1662, a pious woman was taken
with "strange fits." She had "extremely violent bodily motions," often
during church services. Strange voices came from her that were clearly
not her own. These voices accused several other women. One, a "lewd,
ignorant and considerably aged woman," confessed that she had been
familiar with the Devil, even that he "had frequent use of her body with
much seeming (but indeed horrible, hellish) delight to her." This woman
was hanged in 1663.

The most celebrated outbreak of witchcraft in colonial America was
at Salem Village—now Danvers, and the site of a state mental hospital.
The daughter of a Puritan clergyman of Salem Village was afflicted, as
well as his niece who lived with them. The contagion spread to several
of their friends. All, girls between 9 and 20 years, accused several of
their elders of bewitching them. When testifying in court they went into
fits during which they were "dreadfully tortured and tormented." The
mother of one of the girls soon had a seizure also: "She was so stiff she

could not be bended" at first, then she "began to strive violently with her arms and legs," her mouth was drawn to one side, all continuing for nearly half an hour. The outcome of the witch trials is only too familiar. Nineteen men and women died—none were burned, but 18 were hanged and one man was pressed to death with heavy stones for refusing to testify. These executions took place between July 19 and September 22, 1692.

Soon after September 22, citizens and judges began to doubt the legality and efficacy of their measures. There were no more witchcraft trials or executions then or ever afterward in New England. In 1706 Ann Putnam, whose mother's condition I have just described, stood up in the parish church while the clergyman read her contrite words: "I desire to be humbled before God. It was a great delusion of Satan that deceived me in that sad time." In Europe executions for witchcraft continued throughout the 18th century. The last in Great Britain was in 1722, in Switzerland in 1782, and in Poland in 1793.

From these instances of superstitious fear—many others could be mentioned throughout these centuries everywhere in Europe—it should not be supposed that all men shared these beliefs and accepted persecutions. Long before, in the Canon Episcopi, a collection of ecclesiastical decrees made about 906 A.D., a remarkably enlightened view had been expressed. Denounced were the errors of women "seduced by the illusions or phantasms of demons ... For Satan ... deludes the minds of his subjects in sleep, so that the victim believes that these things, which only the spirit experiences, she really experiences in the body." Kittredge says of this passage: (6) "If this had been consistently applied throughout the witch persecutions ... the Witches' Sabbath would have been relegated to the domain of disordered intellects and bad dreams."

E. The Enlightenment: Soon after the printing of the *Malleus Malificarum,* medical men and scholars on the Continent and in Great Britain opposed the persecutions, showing recognition that the victims were either guiltless or sick. In 1518 a German physician, Cornelius Agrippa, while serving as town orator in Metz, in Lorraine, came in conflict with the church by defending a woman accused of witchcraft. In 1563 Johannes Weyer, another German physician, wrote that the performances ascribed to witches were mainly impossible and that the witches themselves were deluded. Believing thoroughly in Satan and his demons, he said that the witches were possessed by devils who made them believe that they had entered into compacts with Satan or ridden through the air on broomsticks. Following his lead, the British scholar, Reginald Scot, in a book published in 1584, wrote that the phenomena of witchcraft were due to legerdemain of the kind practised by jugglers, deceptive to audiences only too ready to see what they wished to believe. But these efforts had little influence either on beliefs or on persecution. No less a person than King James the First, of England, denounced the "damnable opinions" of Weyer and Scot in a book called, *Daemonologie,* appearing in 1616. It was not till the beginning of the 18th century that the execution of witches ceased in England. Two contributors to this fortunate outcome were Meric Casaubon and John Webster. Casaubon's book, published in 1655, was entitled, *A Treatise Concerning Enthusiasm, as it is an Effect of Nature: but is mistaken by Many for Either Divine Inspiration, or Diabolical Possession.* He describes a visit to a man who was supposed to be possessed and decided that he was suffering from some bodily distemper. Though Webster, whose book appeared in 1677, believed in angels, devils and witches, he asserted that witches, misled by demons, did their work by poisons and other natural means. His dedicatory epistle addresses five Yorkshire justices of the peace, warning them of the necessity of distinguishing between imposters and those unfortunate persons who are "under a mere passive delusion" that they are witches. He counsels the magistrates not to believe impossible confessions. A distinguished lawyer named Roger North, described the women appearing before the court at Exeter in 1682, as "very old, decrepit and impotent ... wretched old creatures" ... persecuted with noise and fury by the rabble.

In Massachusetts, Thomas Brattle, in a letter of 1692 regarding the Salem Village confessing witches, wrote that they were: "deluded, imposed upon, and under the influence of some evil spirit; and therefore unfit to be evidences either against themselves, or anyone else." (7) Thanks to the courage and good sense of these men and others like them, the persecutions of witches ended finally in Europe and America.

F. Questions: Several questions remain to be considered. The first is: what kind of people were the witches and their accusers? Evidence for psychopathology on both sides is clear. Several of the cases given in the *Malleus Malificarum* were hysterics suffering from pseudocyesis, impotence, tics, or paralysis. The women who invited punishment by openly breaking the law or by incriminating themselves may have been psychotic depressives indulging in self-condemnation or having delusions demanding punishment. Schizophrenics still occasionally believe themselves to be possessed by devils. The masochism of the victims of persecution and the sadism of their persecutors seem evident enough. Many of the clergymen and judges, however, do not seem sadistic so much as dogmatic and self-righteous men under a kind of mass delusion or psychosis of association which overcame whole regions in times of fanaticism and wide-spread fear. It is the recognition of this phenomenon that has led writers to call some recent epidemics of political persecution "witch-hunts." When the witch-persecutions were at their height, hysterical epidemics such as the dancing mania of northern Europe and the tarantism of Italy were also prevalent. (8). From Roger North's description, it is reasonable to suppose that many victims were senile or pre-senile, perhaps mental defectives or old schizophrenics as well. In Salem Village the girls, reacting perhaps to the rigid discipline, religious dogmatism, and sexual repression of that Puritan town, may have accused their elders as a way of expressing their hatred and rebellion—manifestations of the generation gap in their time.

A second question is: why should this prolonged outbreak of fear and persecution have come when it did? Men had believed in witches and witchcraft for centuries, possession by demons had been spoken of at least since Jesus' time. It was only between the 15th and 18th centuries that thousands were executed.

Three possible answers come to mind. The first is that suggested by Rosen (9), that the two most important examples of collective psychopathology which took place in Medieval and Resaissance Europe—psychic epidemics (such as flagellations and religious enthusiasms) and particularly witch hunting, are the results of stresses and tensions—virulent plagues, other epidemics, long cold winters and widespread floods. These inspired fear, uncertainty, and suspicion. Eventually people found reasons for these calamities in their irrational beliefs. An atmosphere characterized by constant threat of violence and death, by the uncertainty of the frontier, and by lack of other emotional outlets fostered psychic epidemics in America. It is true that the Black Death raged through Europe in the 14th century, killing more than half the population in some regions. In the latter half of the 17th century the plague swept through Europe again, striking London in 1666. Though the fear of witches aroused widespread panic, the plague is not mentioned to my knowledge in the *Malleus Malificarum.* Reginald Scot, according to Kittredge, speaks of the plague only once, with reference to an Italian case of 1536 in which it was alleged that 40 conspirators tried to start the plague afresh by smearing doors and doorposts with a deadly ointment. Other authors do not bring up the subject at all. Mora supposes a relationship between tarantism and the ancient Dionysian possessions, described in Euripedes *Bacchae,* still dormant after 1500 years in Southern Italy, the ancient Magna Graecia. This is an intriguing theory, but can hardly account for irrational behavior in northern and eastern Europe, or in America, so far from possible Grecian remnants.

A characteristic of the writers of the Malleus, and of many other persecutors of witches, is their virulent hatred and abject fear of women—at least of "wicked" women. One can imagine two possible origins for this attitude. During the middle ages the position of women among the upper classes, at least in theory, rose considerably through the institution of chivalry or knighthood. The church at the time was strictly patriarchal. Despite its veneration for the Virgin and despite the canonization of women saints and the founding of nunneries, the male sex ruled in the church as elsewhere. The secular veneration of women challenged this patriarchal masculine supremacy and may have aroused fears within the ecclesiastical hierarchy. More likely is the hypothesis that priests feared their own sexual impulses, especially when stimulated by immoral and hysterical women. The castigation of "drabs and whores" and the descriptions of the sexual antics and practices of witches support this view.

A third possible answer is the rise of Protestantism. Until the 15th century the church had been successful in crushing heretical movement that had arisen in Western Europe. The Albigensians, for example, in southern France, had been extirpated in the 12th and 13th centuries. In the 15th century, however, in Germany, Switzerland and Britain rebellion against the power of Rome could not be suppressed. So the church turned its attention to those insane, neurotic, and senile people, as well as those who were perhaps heirs of an ancient tradition of genuine witchcraft, who could not defend themselves. If a priest could leave to marry and express his sexual needs openly, how much more urgent was it to suppress temptations offered by seductive women? In the 16th century, during the Counter-Reformation, the Roman church enforced more rigidly its rules regarding celibacy than it had in previous centuries, in order to solidify its opposition to Protestantism. This made life harder for a priest. In Puritan and Calvinist England and Scotland, as well as in America, though marriage was allowed the clergy, sexual morality was considerably tightened, especially for the young. Hence the great prevalence of hysteria.

A last question is: from what unconscious source did these aberrations come? We are accustomed to thinking that the unconscious mind contains mostly sexual and aggressive fantasies and impulses. The witches and their persecutors had full measure of those, as the case histories quoted clearly demonstrate. Now we recognize a more archaic level of the unconscious. often expressed in schizophrenia: the level of the magical. After 200 years of rationalism this level is more deeply repressed in most of us than it was before. We have to go to isolated areas of the United States, or to "under-developed" countries, to find it close to the surface, as it was in the days of witchcraft persecution. Arnold Ludwig writes (10) about symptoms of bewitchment among the Spanish-Americans of southern Colorado. He finds, with Ernest Jones, that such cases often suffered from guilt associated with forbidden incestuous wishes. He also found cases with forbidden homosexual wishes, aggressive wishes or impulses, unmet dependency needs, and feelings of inadequacy. One common feature he saw beyond all of these was the absolution that the belief in witchcraft gave from guilt, by projection of blame onto an external agent. The devil, demon or witch became a convenient scapegoat. The scapegoat itself comes from the Old Testament (Leviticus 16:20-28): "And Aaron shall lay both his hands upon the head of the live goat, and confess over him all the iniquities of the children of Israel, and all their transgressions and sins, putting them upon the head of the goat, and shall send him away ... into the wilderness." It is always the minority who serves as a scapegoat—in this case the psychotic and the neurotic who were despised, misunderstood and feared. As always, they suffered and were sacrificed. The persecutors actually feared their own imaginings.

We can say that mental illness and neurosis were widely prevalent in the late Middle Ages and throughout the Renaissance. Their nature was little recognized except by isolated physicians and scholars. Objectivity and compassion were obscured by superstition and fanaticism. Except for a few instances to be mentioned in the next chapter, treatment similar to what we use today was seldom given. Exorcism by representatives of the church was practised. Though it may have helped many, it was presumably unused for most of those who needed help.

BIBLIOGRAPHY

1. The English Bible, King James version, I Sam. 16;14-23; 17;7-12.

2. Ibid, Daniel 4;30-36.

3. Ibid, Mark 5;1-19

4. *Malleus Malificarum,* translated by Rev. Montague Summers, Pushkin Press, London, 1928.

5. (a) Chadwick Hansen, *Witchcraft at Salem,* Brazeller, New York, 1969.
   (b) Marion L. Starky, *The Devil in Massachusetts,* Knopf, New York, 1950.

6. George Lyman Kittridge, *Witchcraft in Old and New England,* Russell and Russell, New York, 1929 and 1956, p. 244.

7. For this and preceding references see Kittredge, op. cit. 399 ff. etc.

8. George Mora, *An Historical and Sociopsychiatric Appraisal of Tarantism, etc.,* Bulletin of the History of Medicine, 37, 417, 1963.

9. G. Rosen, *Psychopathology in the Social Process,* J. Health and Human Behavior, 1:200, 1960. Also, G. Rosen, *Madness in Society,* University of Chicago Press, Chicago, 1968.

10. Arnold M. Ludwig, *Witchcraft Today,* Diseases of the Nerv. Syst., 26:288, 1965.

Chapter 3

INSTITUTIONAL PSYCHIATRY

Introduction. In Renaissance times most mental patients who were not hanged or burned at the stake, or who did not respond to exorcism, roamed the countryside or were kept at home.

In successive centuries in Western Europe various expedients were tried to handle the problem offered by these and other outcasts. From about the 14th century, a few hundred mental patients were boarded in peasants' homes in Gheel, Belgium. This town had a shrine to St. Dymphna, who was martyred (the legend goes) while trying to escape from the incestuous attention of her royal father. Mental patients are still housed in Gheel, under state supervision. The Arabs, the most enlightened people in medieval Europe, built a number of asylums for their mentally sick—the last in Grenada in 1365 (1). Before the days of witch-hunting, Father Jofre founded the first Christian asylum in Spain in 1410 (2). The first mental hospital in the New World was opened in Mexico City in 1566 (3). Santa Maria di Pieta was founded in Rome in 1570. These institutions, though memorable historically, took care of very few of those in need.

As towns grew bigger, the burden of the sick grew greater. By the 17th century a new policy had grown up in Europe. Inability or unwillingness to work being judged a crime, all vagrants were rounded up and placed in large institutions in the cities. Included in the catch were mental defectives, petty criminals, prostitutes, beggars, and the insane. Foucault (4) calls this "The Great Confinement." One of the first of such places was the General Hospital in Paris, founded in 1656. Similar institutions were soon opened in Germany and Switzerland. The Bethlem Royal Hospital in London, founded in 1547, was transformed into such a hospital. It soon was called "Bedlam," notorious in the 18th century as a place for society folk to be amused by the inmates' antics. Hogarth immortalized Bedlam in a painting. Elsewhere in England workhouses were established, until manufacturers objected to the competition of cheap pauper labor. The work was then taken away, and workhouses became almshouses, for the idle poor and sick. Since religion forbade killing them or totally neglecting them they were kept alive and cared for after a fashion. As they could neither support themselves, pay taxes, nor add to the common wealth, expenditure on their keep was kept to a bare minimum. Since most believed that the insane and feeble-minded could feel no pain and, like Nebuchadnezzar, lived at the level of animals, the hospitals were unheated and the inmates hardly clothed. They slept on straw. If obstreperous, they were confined in cages, or chained to the walls. They were believed to be incurable. Death under these conditions was merciful.

St. Vincent dePaul. The honor of changing this dismal policy, by initiating the humane care of the mentally ill, is shared by several countries. In 1632 St. Vincent dePaul was given charge of St. Lazare Hospital in France (5). Finding a number of insane in buildings towards the back of the grounds, he took them in his special charge, treating them with humanity and compassion. He trained Sisters of Charity, led by Louise de Marillac, to care for the women patients. They continued their work till their deaths in the same year, 1660.

Chiarugi. Italy was the birthplace of Vincenzo Chiarugi. When the Hospital of Bonifasio was opened in Florence in 1788, he was put in charge of the mental patients. The following year, in the new hospital's regulations, he decreed that physical force was never to be used and restraint was to be only temporary. He wrote: "It is a supreme moral duty and medical obligation to respect the insane individual as a person. It is especially necessary for the person who treats the mental patient to gain his confidence and trust. It is best therefore to be tactful and understanding ... in a kind way. The attitude of doctors and nurses must be authoritative and impressive, but at the same time pleasant."(6) He directed the hospital according to these principles until his death in 1820.

Pinel. Philippe Pinel was a young French provincial physician when, in his own words, "the loss of a friend, who became insane through excessive love of glory in 1783" (7), turned his mind toward psychiatry. For five years he was attending physician to a small mental hospital. In 1793 he was appointed chief physician to the national asylum, Bicêtre, in Paris. He was unfavorably impressed with his new charge. "The halls and passages were much confined ... the cold of winter and heat of summer equally intolerable and injurious. The rooms were exceedingly small. Baths, we had none ... nor had we extensive liberties for walking, gardening or other exercises." But he found in the layman in charge, Citizen Pussin, a man who exercised toward all "the vigilance of a kind and affectionate parent, mild and at the same time inflexibly firm." Building on the foundation begun by this excellent man, Pinel put in practice "the maxims of enlightened humanity." The aides were "not allowed on any pretext whatever, to strike a madman ... strait waistcoats, superior force and seclusion for a limited time, were the only punishments inflicted." (8) As much as revolutionary times permitted, he supplied wholesome food, warmth, and adequate clothing. He applied the conventional remedies of medicine in those days—bleeding, leeches, emesis, purging, and nauseating medications but only if psychological methods failed. In short, he used the methods of "moral treatment"—"moral" meaning, in the words of his pupil Esquirol, "the application of ... intelligence and of emotions" in the treatment of mental illness.

In 1794 Pinel was appointed head of the Bicetre's sister institution, the Salpêtrière, and, soon after, professor in the School of Medicine at the University of Paris. In 1788 the Salpêtrière had been thus described: "the largest hospital in Paris and possibly in Europe ... both a house for women and a prison. It receives pregnant women and girls ... young girls of all ages, aged married men and women, raving lunatics, imbeciles, paralytics, blind persons, cripples ... uncurables of all sorts." In 1792, when the revolutionaries did away with arbitrary imprisonment, many of these were discharged, but the insane, the defective, and epileptic remained. Pinel applied to these patients the same principles and methods he had found so successful at the Bicêtre. He devoted himself to their study with fresh eyes. "I regularly took notes of whatever appeared deserving of my attention and compared what I thus collected, with facts analogous to them that I met with in books, or amongst my own memoranda of former dates." (9) He classified their conditions in a simple fashion; he compiled statistics of incidence and of response to treatment and causes of death; he wrote articles and books.

Here is a case from the second edition of his text book, illustrating his interest in immediate causes:

> "A young man, distinguished by his talents and his profound knowledge of chemistry, contemplated for some time a discovery which ought, in his mind, to lead to a huge fortune. His imagination expanding, he decided to stay for several days shut up in his laboratory. In order to stimulate working, banish sleep, and to lift himself up to the level of the project he contemplated, he prepared several kinds of stimulants. First a young singer shared his retreat, second, he repeatedly made use of strong liquor, third, he sniffed from time to time various odorous substances, and finally he sprinkled his laboratory simultaneously with eau de Cologne. Imagine how the combined action of all these, together with the heat of a furnace, was apt to carry to the highest degree of excitement all his physical and mental faculties, and you will not be the least astonished if, in about a week, he lapsed into a most furious delirium." (10)

Pinel became a legend in his own time. First, Frenchmen, then physicians and philanthropists from all over Europe came to observe and to study. His book was translated into several languages and read in America as well as throughout Europe. He trained pupils to carry on his methods.

After Pinel's death in 1826 his most eminent disciple, J.E.D. Esquirol, carried on his work in France.

In his treatise, Pinel quotes a number of British physicians who had written on mental illness. They made much of the need for establishing one's authority over one's patients at the outset by, for example, fixing them with one's gaze and staring them down. A humane superintendent at Bethlem Hospital had forbidden sight-seeing for a fee some years before.

William Battie. The first English physician to care humanely for the mentally ill was William Battie. In 1750, after eight years as a governor of Bethlem Royal, he founded St. Luke's Hospital nearby. In an appeal for funds made that year are these words: "There must be servants peculiarly qualified, and every patient must have a separate room, and diet ... equal to persons in health." In 1753 Dr. Battie took pupils in his hospital—the first attempt in England to instruct students by actual observation of mental patients. In 1758 he published *A Treatise on Madness.* There we find these enlightened opinions: "Madness is ... as manageable as many other distempers, which are equally dreadful and obstinate, and yet are not looked upon as incurable ... such unhappy objects ought by no means to be abandoned, much less shut up in loathesome prisons ... Madness ... rejects all general methods, e.g., bleeding, blisters, caustics, rough cathartics, the gums and fetid anti-hysterics, ... and vomits. ... Nor is the lancet when applied to the feeble and convulsed lunatic, less destructive than a sword." He added: "Whenever upon sufficient trial not only of vomits but even of rougher purges ... the patient grows worse or at least gains no ground, they are all entirely to be laid aside ... many a lunatic, who by the repetition of vomits and other convulsive stimuli would have been strained into downright idiotism, has when given over as incurable, recovered his understanding." (11).

The Retreat at York. In 1790 a Quaker was confined in the York County Asylum in England. She died in a few weeks. Her relatives had been denied permission to see her. Soon after several members of the York Friends Meeting proposed the founding of a hospital of their own. Among them was William Tuke, a tea merchant. In 1792 Tuke laid a proposal before the meeting for a "retired habitation ... for the numbers of our society and others ... who may be in a state of lunacy." In 1796 the Retreat of York opened its doors. They have not been closed since.

In this quiet Retreat drugs were found to be of little benefit, compared to warm baths, liberal diet, suitable amusements, and sober reading. Neither chains nor flogging was permitted and restraints were seldom used. Fresh air and gardening were prescribed. Soon the Retreat's reputation grew and visitors came from everywhere in Europe and America.

The York Asylum heard more of the Retreat in 1813. Samuel Tuke, William's grandson, published that year his *Description of the Retreat.* Alarmed, Dr. Charles Best, the superintendent of the Asylum, accused Tuke of defamation. In October Samuel Tuke and twelve other leading citizens went to a meeting of the governors, paid their dues, and forced the setting up of a committee of inquiry. In August, 1814, every officer, keeper, and nurse was removed, and Dr. Best resigned. The managers of the Retreat took over the running of the Asylum till a new staff was found.

In May, 1814, a similar committee of Londoners visited Bethlem Royal Hospital. What they found led to the appointment of a parliamentary committee which inquired into Bethlem, the York Asylum, and workhouses, and private "madhouses" throughout England. Their report appeared in 1815, followed in the next two years by reports on the conditions of the "lunatic poor" in Scotland and Ireland. Not until 1828 were acts of parliament passed amending the laws of 1774 regarding the erection and regulation of county asylums. Meanwhile conditions at Bethlem had much improved (11).

According to Hunter and Macalpine, the mental illness from which George III suffered had much to do with stimulating public interest in and concern for the mentally ill poor (12).

Conolly. John Conolly "triumphantly completed the work" of Pinel and Tuke. His son-in-law, Henry Maudsley, himself a celebrated psychiatrist, wrote that Conolly "not only enforced a certain improved system of practice, but he expounded the humane and scientific theory of it ... He not only made the hitherto obscure movement a world known success, but he made reaction impossible." Born in 1794 in Lincolnshire, he graduated in medicine at Edinburgh in 1821. He visited the Salpêtrière in Paris and talked with Esquirol. He lectured on mental diseases at the University of London, and wrote a book, *The Indications of Insanity,* published in 1830. His practical experience began in 1839, when he was appointed physician at the Pauper Lunatic Asylum at Hanwell, near London. He had recommended less confinement, individualized moral treatment, and more communication between specialists in mental disease and other doctors. At Hanwell he soon put into effect the method for which he became famous, that of non-restraint. Not only were patients not to be chained or flogged, they were not to be restrained in any way (within the walls of the hospital) no matter how active or excited or potentially dangerous they were. No straitjackets were permitted. Though most psychiatrists of his time thought he was too radical in his permissiveness, his example went far to reduce the number of mental patients mechanically restrained in all hospitals (13).

In America the Pennsylvania Hospital in Philadelphia, dating from 1751, was built with provisions for mental patients. The first state hospital in the American colonies was founded at Williamsburg, Virginia, in 1773. From that date until 1862 this hospital was directed by a member of the Galt family—five in all.

Rush. The first physician in America who could be called a psychiatrist was Benjamin Rush of Philadelphia. He treated mental patients at Pennsylvania Hospital after getting his medical degree in Edinburgh in 1768. He was active in revolutionary politics, a friend of Franklin, Jefferson, and Adams and a signer of the Declaration of Independence. He invented a chair into which excited patients could be strapped. "It acts as a sedative to the tongue and temper as well as to the blood vessels. In 24, 12, 6 and in some cases in 4 hours, the most refractory patients have been composed. I have called it a tranquillizer." In 1812, the year before his death, he published the first American textbook of psychiatry. "The cause of madness," he wrote, "is seated primarily in the blood vessels of the brain." (14) He recognized exciting causes, however, acting either directly on the brain, such as injuries, tumors, and apoplexy, or upon the whole body, such as fever, famine, excessive ardent spirits, and inordinate sexual desires and gratifications. He discovered four cases of madness in young men, between 1804 and 1807, which he blamed on "onanism," or masturbation. "The morbid effects of intemperance in sexual intercourse with women are feeble, and of transient nature, compared with the train of physical and moral evils which this solitary vice fixes upon the body and mind." He also incriminated mental causes such as intense study, and strong emotions like joy, anger, terror, love, and grief. He told of the sad case of "a player (who) destroyed himself in Philadelphia in the year 1803, soon after being hissed off the stage." Two persons killed themselves immediately after drawing high prizes in a lottery. In discussing treatment, Rush advises that the physician be uniformly dignified, have strict regard to truth and "acquire the obedience and affection of his deranged patients by acts of kindness." "They seldom forget three things after their recovery," he said, "acts of cruelty, acts of indignity, and acts of kindness." Yet he did advise, where other means failed, coercion (by the straitjacket or by his tranquilizing chair), privation of food, cold showers, or the threat of drowning. He recommended bleeding (but not leeches), purging, emetics, and blisters, in order to effect a transfer of violent madness from the brain to the lower limbs and then out of the body, reminiscent of ancient Egypt. Regarding dreams he wrote: "A dream may be considered as a transient paroxysm of delirium and delirium as a permanent dream." He proposed the establishment of a United States Peace Office, with the figures of a lamb, a dove and an olive branch over the door, together with the inscription, "Peace on Earth—Good Will to Man."

Another Quaker and Philadelphian interested in mental disorder was Thomas Scattergood. He visited York and dined with William Tuke at the Retreat in 1799. When, in 1811, a committee was formed by the Philadelphia Friends Yearly Meeting "to make provision for such of our members as may be deprived of the use of their reason," Scattergood's name was first. In 1813 land was bought and 1817 Friends Hospital was opened. Moral treatment was provided much as at the Retreat at York. The precepts of the little book written by Samuel Tuke of York were scrupulously followed (15).

Friends Hospital was the first of a number of private institutions founded within the next few years. Thomas Eddy, a New York Quaker, also read Samuel Tuke's little book. He persuaded the Board of the New York Hospital to open a branch devoted to the treatment of the mentally ill. McLean Hospital near Boston and the Hartford Retreat (now the "Institute of Living") soon followed.

Kirkbride. A resident physician at Friends in 1832 and 1833 was Dr. Thomas Kirkbride. When in 1840 Pennsylvania Hospital wished to open up a separate department for mental patients he was called to be its superintendent. Dr. Kirkbride believed in the "value of employment in the treatment of insanity ... The object is to restore mental health and tranquilize the restlessness and mitigate the sorrows of disease. Drawing and painting were taught by an artist from the city. Several patients gave instruction to others on the same ward in different branches of learning ... these were lectures on astronomy, electricity, physiology, optical illusions, and the wonders of nature and of Egypt." (16) Recognized as an architect, he designed a building to give the most light and air with the most protection from noise, that was widely copied throughout the country. He called a meeting of mental hospital superintendents in 1844, from which sprang the "American Psychiatric Association." Dr. Galt of Williamsburg was among them.

Dorothea L. Dix. Kirkbride entertained at his hospital in 1844 that remarkable woman, Dorothea Lynde Dix. A Massachusetts teacher and a Unitarian, she had discovered while teaching a Sunday School class in a Boston prison, that mental patients were confined there. This started her on a career of founding mental hospitals—in Massachusetts, Rhode

Island, New Jersey, Pennsylvania, and many other states. She induced the Congress in Washington to find money to build St. Elizabeth's Hospital. After a hospital was opened, she frequently returned to make sure it was running right—a one-woman inspection committee. During the Civil War she had charge of nursing in the Union Armies. She died at Trenton State Hospital in New Jersey, a guest of that grateful institution (17).

The Cycles of Reform. The history of psychiatric institutions in this country is one of stagnation followed by reform, one cycle succeeding the other over and over. First there was the period of initial enthusiasm, when many private hospitals were founded. Then with the realization that there were thousands of patients not being reached by the private institutions, many state hospitals were opened, on the moral treatment model. Taking Worcester State Hospital in Massachusetts as an example (18), between its founding in 1832, and 1852, it had a census of only 200 to 300 patients. The recovery or marked improvement rate in patients ill less than a year was about 70 per cent. In the second half of the century immigrants began to pour in from all over Europe. In the hospital report of 1854 they are first mentioned: "The hospital was fast becoming a hospital for Irish immigrants rather than for the intelligent yeomanry of Massachusetts who could pay their board." It was suggested that New Englanders and immigrants be segregated—though both were white and English-speaking! By 1902 the hospital had 1000 patients and by 1950, 2500. Most immigrants had a high incidence of mental illness presumably because of the stresses of poverty and of adaptation to a new land. Hospital personnel were overwhelmed, physically and emotionally. The institutions changed from home-like havens of moral treatment to huge custodial asylums. Each physician was supposed to take care of over 200 patients rather than less than 100 as before. The opinion grew that such patients could not appreciate good surroundings and were mostly incurable due to poor heredity or some organic defect. The proportion of patients markedly improved went down to 5 per cent in the 1930's. The impersonality of urban life was reflected in the depersonalization of the state hospital patient.

Despite all rationalizations, this relapse to the conditions before Pinel did not go entirely unnoticed. At the turn of the century the psychologist William James deplored the fatalistic insensitivity of legislators and hospital officials. At an annual meeting of the American Psychiatric Association Dr. S. Weir Mitchell, the Philadelphia neurologist and novelist, was asked to speak. He upbraided the hospital superintendents in a similar fashion. The "National Mental Hygiene Association" was founded after Clifford W. Beers had dislosed in his book, *A Mind That Found Itself,* (19) the sad conditions in a Connecticut State Hospital. In the early 20th century, research and teaching hospitals were opened adjacent to medical schools, at Ann Arbor, in Boston, and in Baltimore. Out-patient clinics and child guidance centers were organized in order to treat patients before they had to be hospitalized—secondary prevention, we call it now. The sale of liquor was forbidden and laws passed against the sale and use of drugs, in order to prevent alcoholic psychoses and drug addiction.

Thanks to two World Wars and an economic depression, the State hospitals were again at a low ebb by 1945. We are now in the midst of another wave of reform. The changes are being made at two levels: first, medically, and second, administratively. Penicillin has largely done away with psychosis due to syphilis, and electro-convulsive therapy has shortened the duration of psychotic depressions as well as prevented many suicides. Since 1955 tranquilizers and antidepressants have done wonders for many schizophrenics and the milder depressions. The organization of community mental centers and half-way houses has allowed the state hospital administrators to discharge large numbers of long-term patients, not to admit so many new patients, and so to reduce hospital populations to manageable numbers. Private hospitals and psychiatric departments of general hospitals take care of many of the acutely ill. Immigration no longer is so overwhelming. "Moral treatment" can again be applied.

Summary. We have seen that psychotic patients, before the days of hospitals, were outlawed and neglected. They were hidden at home or driven out of their communities into the countryside. From the 15th century, a few were placed in religious institutions as examples and for the moral edification of the pious. In the 17th century they were punished, abused or restrained after being herded into huge general hospitals or work houses. When moral treatment began, the patients were treated with benevolent authority. Physical conditions were much better and kindness much more often shown, but the patients were often treated like children. They were given little choice regarding their treatment or their future. In the next phase, they were depersonalized in over-crowded or under-staffed mental hospitals, subjects for studies in classification, prognosis, or biochemistry. We are now entering the "humanizing" era, where patients are considered to be potentially responsible adults and treated accordingly. Enlightened and humanitarian men and women have always looked at patients so. This outlook is becoming public policy.

BIBLIOGRAPHY

1. George Mora, From Demonology to the Narrenturm, in *Historic Derivations of Modern Psychiatry,* ed., by Iago Galdston, McGraw-Hill, New York, 1967.

2. R. B. Rumbaut, The First Psychiatric Hospital in the Western World, *Am. J. of Psychiat.* 128:1305, 1972.

3. Bernadino Alvarez: New World Psychiatric Pioneer, *A. J. P.* 127:1217, 1971.

4. Michel Foucault, *Madness and Civilization,* Pantheon, New York, 1965.

5. Sister Mary E. Walsh, Saint Vincent dePaul—Ste. Louise deMarillac and their daughters, *Amer. J. Psychiatry,* 102:198, 1945.

6. George Mora, A Precursor of Modern Hospital Treatment, *Mental Hospitals:* 10:23, 1959.

7. George Rosen, *Madness in Society,* Univ. of Chicago Press, Chicago, p. 164.

8. Philippe Pinel, *A Treatise on Insanity,* translated by D. D. Davis, Sheffield, 1806, reprinted by Hafner Pub. Co., New York, 1962.

9. E. T. Carlson and N. Dain. The Psychotherapy that was Moral Treatment, *Am. J. of Psychiatry,* 117:519, 1960.

10. Philippe Pinel, *Traite Medico-Philosophique sur L'Alienation Mentale,* 2nd edition, Paris, 1809.

11. Richard Hunter and Ida Macalpine, *Three Hundred Years of Psychiatry,* Oxford U. Press, London, 1963.

12. Ida Macalpine and Richard Hunter, *George III and the Mad Business,* Pantheon, New York, 1969.

13. John Conolly, *The Indications of Insanity,* with an introduction by Richard Hunter and Ida Macalpine, London, 1964.

14. Benjamin Rush, *Medical Inquiries and Observations Upon the Diseases of the Mind,* reprinted by Hafner Publishing Co., New York, 1962.

15. R. A. Clark, Quakers and Psychiatry, *Friends Journal,* Phila., June 6 and June 13, 1959.

16. Earl D. Bond, *Dr. Kirkbride and his Mental Hospital,* Lippincott, Phila., 1937.

17. Helen E. Marshall, *Dorothea Dix,* U. of N. Carolina Press, Chapel Hill, 1937.

18. J. S. Bockoven, *Moral Treatment in American Psychiatry,* Springer, New York, 1963.

19. Clifford W. Beers, *A Mind that Found Itself,* Longmans Green, New York, 1908 (4th edition, 1917).

Chapter 4

ACADEMIC PSYCHIATRY IN EUROPE AND AMERICA

Introduction. Psychiatry as a specialty was born in institutions. The aim of the pioneers was primarily administrative. They were concerned with the management of patients and the governing and architecture of hospitals. They seldom concerned themselves with causes, except for immediate and precipitating ones. They were not theoretical, but practical men.

The ancients found two sources of mental illness: the spiritual, from the gods or from demons, and the human, arising within the sufferer himself. These inner causes were either psychological—from pride, jealousy, or shame; or they were physiological—from the body humors, or from the brain itself. Academic psychiatry rejected spiritual causation. At first it could not decide on the relative importance of the psychological and the physiological. These two views struggled for ascendance in the first decades of the 19th century. Finally the physiological outlook largely won out. Benjamin Rush illustrated this conflict. For him, disease in the blood vessels of the brain were the ultimate source of insanity; but he recognized the importance of fear, grief, love, and other strong emotions as proximate causes.

Returning to Europe, we find three principal sources of the impetus toward the organic explanation for insanity: phrenology, pathology and the study of heredity. That seminal decade, the final one in the 18th century, also gave birth in Vienna to phrenology. Like mesmerism, which also originated in Vienna, it was accused of charlatanism. Yet both led to important theoretical and therapeutic advances.

Phrenology. The founder of phrenology was Franz Joseph Gall. Born in Baden, Germany, in 1758, he began the practice of medicine in Vienna in 1785. He became convinced that differences in temperament and talent among men were reflected in differences in the development of portions of the brain. He concluded that these anatomical differences could be detected by examining the surface of the skull. His first publication in the new "science" of phrenology was in 1791, his first lectures in 1796: encompassing the years when Pinel began his work in Paris and Tuke his work in England. At first his doctrines met with great success—so great that in 1802 the Austrian government forbade him to lecture on the grounds that his teaching was dangerous to religion. By then he had gained his most prominent disciple, J. K. Spurzheim. They shortly left Austria for

England. Gall's lectures in London were not as successful as those in Vienna. Spurzheim set up a psychiatric practice. In fact, in 1817, he published an excellent psychiatric text, in which phrenology plays a very small part (1). Here are those paragraphs describing the application of phrenology to the understanding of mental illness:

> "It is a fact, that by far the greatest number of those who are insane by pride have the organ of self-esteem large in proportion to the other organs of the mind. It does not follow, however, that everyone who has this organ large must become insane by pride, nor that everyone who has this organ small will be absolutely exempt from such an hallucination; for every small organ may be excited by diseased affection, and show too great activity and deranged manifestations. The influence of the size seems to be obvious, since the greatest number of persons, insane with peculiar hallucinations, have the respective organs larger. Gall possesses the skull of a madman, from amativeness, who fancied himself husband to six wives, and manifested various ideas of that kind. His cerebellum was extremely large. Gall has also the skull of a woman who imagined herself pregnant with five children: the organ of the love of offspring is of extraordinary development.

> But I repeat, that only in the greater number of cases, not always, the respective organs will be found larger, in the same way as the predominant character is mostly, but not always, preserved. Particularly in those who, when young, adult, and insane, manifest great energy of the same dispositions, the respective organs will be found large ...

> Thus, in insanity, the configuration of heads is neither to be overlooked, nor to be over-rated.

Though phrenology is now thoroughly discredited, in its day it served to popularize the doctrines that the brain is the organ of the mind and that different functions belong to different areas of the brain. Discounting the claim that the skull surface was significant, anatomists and neurophysiologists studied the functions and connections of the cerebral lobes themselves. By the end of the century, thanks to Paul Broca and others, it was recognized that broader areas had wider functions than Gall and Spurzheim thought they discerned. Vision, hearing, smell, motor activity, speech, and abstract thought each had a large section. As microscopic anatomy developed, each area was found to have a characteristic set of layers and cell distribution. The study of speech disorders—the aphasias—in relation to intellectual defect and the emotions in brain injuries and tumors, was especially illuminating.

Brain Pathology. In the middle of the 19th century came the development of gross and microscopic pathology. Careful study of post-mortem specimens led to the conclusion that each disease had its type of damage to the structure of the affected organs. Rudolf Virchow, for many years professor of pathology at the University of Berlin, investigated the brain as well as other organs. He was a remarkable personality as well as a scientist and teacher. He visited the ruins of Troy with their discoverer, Schliemann. He did research on the anthropology of primitive man in Europe. He was a member of the German Reichstag and architect of the city plan of Berlin. In a whole series of volumes, the first published in 1858, he did more than any other academic man to further the doctrine that disease meant organic change.

Among German psychiatrists of the time, none preached the new doctrine more enthusiastically than Wilhelm Griesinger (2). In 1864 he became director of the psychiatric clinic in Berlin. In the few years remaining to him before his premature death at 51 in 1868, he founded the German *Archives of Psychiatry and Neurology* and became the chief advocate of the "somatic" or organic school of psychiatry. His dictum was "no mental disease without brain disease." This did not mean that he ignored the psychological causes of much mental illness. In fact, as we shall see later, he anticipated some of Freud's chief principles. Still he believed that scientific clarity demanded that psychiatry be securely bound to an anatomical and pathological foundation in order not to be lost in foggy and mystical speculations.

Armed with Griesinger's dictum, university pathologists set about the conquest of the brain just as they had overcome so much ignorance with respect to other organs of the body. They made rapid progress at first. One psychosis after another was shown to have characteristic neuropathological changes, correlating with the clinical findings. The names of the researchers are familiar to students of neuroanatomy and of clinical psychiatry because they are preserved in the names of areas of the central nervous system or of disease syndromes. Meynert, Westphal, Wernicke, Korsakoff, Alzheimer and Pick were men who flourished between 1860 and 1918 and who made contributions to the understanding of central nervous system syphilis, alcoholic psychoses, senile and presenile mental disorders. Not content with unraveling the mysteries of such clear cut organic disorders, they often described typical pathological findings in more obscure conditions such as schizophrenia (then called dementia praecox), paranoia, and manic-depressive disorders. Where no microscopic organism or external poison or arterial disease could be found, some obscure toxin or deficiency was hypothesized.

Heredity. Where a definite pathology could not readily be identified, as in the functional disorders, heredity was often invoked. A few rare psychoses were obviously inherited—most notably Huntington's chorea, first described not in Europe, but on Long Island, New York. Extensive research was carried on into the family trees of mental patients for three or four generations. As was expected, it was found that some families were heavily loaded with mental illness, mental defect, criminality, or alcoholism. Years ago everyone learned about the Jukes and the Kallikaks —fictitious names for two American families notorious for the amount of mental and social pathology they spawned, despite their being white, Anglo-Saxon, and Protestant. The twin-study method was later invented. If a disease was inherited, identical twins would presumably both develop it. When someone pointed out that twins were almost always raised by the same parents, records were combed for twins who had been adopted into different homes soon after birth. Such studies have been carried out into the 20th century. Again the investigators triumphantly confirmed their hypothesis: identical twins *did* have a much higher concordance of mental illness and a variety of lesser psychiatric illness. So mental patients, sex deviates, and criminals were often called "degenerate" or "constitutional psychopathic inferiors." Much of the stigma attached to psychiatric illness came from the alleged "hereditary taint" in the families concerned. Mental illness was concealed and the unfortunate victims were hospitalized many miles from home. States passed laws permitting the sterilization of patients or kept them locked up for 20 or 30 years, to prevent them from passing on the illness to descendants.

Types of Physique. Another lead pursued more recently by organicists was the correlation between physique and susceptibility to different functional illnesses. If the shape of the outside of the skull did not give clues to disease or personality, then perhaps the shape of the body would. Ernst Kretschmer was the pioneer in this field, in his book, *Physique and Character,* appearing in 1921. Schizophrenia and schizoid personality were correlated with the asthenic and athletic body types, and manic-depressive illness and cyclothymic personality with the pyknic (or stocky) body type. Allied to this approach was the study of the relationship of the endocrine glands to mental illness. It was well known that the extremes of excess or deprivation of several glandular secretions led to psychosis: the thyroid, adrenals, and others. Perhaps, therefore, there were relationships between body configuration, endocrine function, and personality. Similar reasoning was applied to the relationship between nutrition and psychiatric disorder. Low blood sugar can produce delirium; high blood sugar, coma. Extreme deficiencies in vitamins, especially the various vitamin B fractions, as seen in malnutrition accompanying alcoholism or chronically deficient diets, caused characteristic mental symptoms. Lastly are the psychoses brought on by drugs. It has been known for over 100 years that certain drugs of value in medicine, such as digitalis and atropine, if given in excessive doses will cause delirium. For nearly that long, peyote, the cactus fruit used by American Indians, whose effects were so vividly described in 1896 by S. Weir Mitchell of Philadelphia, (3) has been known to anthropologists. Only very recently have synthetic hallucinogenic drugs been discovered, such as lysergic acid diethylamide, or LSD. The remarkable thing about LSD is that such extraordinarily small quantities can produce mental symptoms. This suggests that a similar substance aberrantly formed in the body would do the same and account for some cases of schizophrenia.

Physical and Physiological Treatments. These and other clinical observations have led to various attempts at treatment of functional mental illness by physical and physiological means. In 1918, Wagner von Jauregg of Vienna observed that paresis (syphilitic psychosis) improved if the patient contracted malarial fever. He infected his hospital patients with malaria, first by means of mosquitoes, then by drawing malarial blood from one paretic and injecting it into another. After a number of paroxysms of fever of 40° or 40.6°C, many of the patients recovered. Since malaria was rather dangerous in itself and several patients died of it, fever was later induced in other ways: by injection of killed typhoid bacilli, or by diathermy, and was found to be equally effective. Since observers had also often noted that schizophrenics sometimes temporarily improved during an incidental bout of febrile illness, psychiatrists in Europe and America gave schizophrenics fever treatment too. In this country, Johns Hopkins School of Medicine was a center for such work. A number of more acutely ill schizophrenics did get well. In Switzerland in the early 1930's Klaesi, at Bern, put excited patients, both manic and schizophrenic, to sleep for 2 or 3 weeks at a time, with a mixture of paraldehyde, barbiturates, or other sedatives. He found this method to be quite effective, though requiring much nursing care. Later in the 1930's two other organic approaches were developed: the insulin-coma treatment by Sakel in Vienna, and the convulsive treatment by Von Meduna in Budapest. While treating excited morphine addicts Sakel observed that their blood sugar levels were above normal. Giving them insulin reduced both their sugar levels and their excitement. Having several schizophrenic patients who were excited, he gave them insulin to calm them. Patients were given 30 to 100 units of insulin 5 or 6 days a week for 30 days. Each day their coma was interrupted after about ½ an hour, by sugar administered by gastric tube or intravenously. Many chronically ill schizophrenics, he claimed, were much better. Von Meduna proposed that there was a natural antagonism between schizophrenia and epilepsy, since he had seen no schizophrenics with seizures and no epileptics with schizophrenia. He therefore produced seizures artificially in schizophrenics by injecting large doses of metrazol, a cardiac stimulant, quickly and intravenously. Acute schizophrenics, he found, were often improved by 20 to 25 such injections. One serious drawback to this treatment was that, before losing consciousness, most patients had a sensation of dying and were, therefore, severely frightened. In the late 1930's in Rome, two Italian physicians, Cerletti and Bini, induced convulsions, first in animals and then in humans, by passing an electric current through the head. Thus was electro-convulsive therapy discovered. It was found to be less frightening and more readily controlled than metrazol treatment. It was also found, contrary to Von Meduna's hypothesis, to be even more effective in depressions than in schizophrenia.

Pharmacotherapy. Meanwhile another organic approach to the understanding and treatment of mental illness was being pursued: the pharmacological. Drugs had been used for centuries in calming mental patients. In the 19th century even opium was used extensively for this purpose. The pharmacological treatment of functional psychosis developed in the past 20 years, first by the discovery of the tranquilizers, then of the antidepressants, and finally of lithium treatment. It is to these advances that we principally owe the unprecedented drop in mental hospital populations.

Since Virchow's time, that is in the past 115 years, great progress has been made in the understanding and treatment of mental illness by means of pathology, physiology, and pharmacology. The duration of illness has been shortened, the severity of symptoms lessened, the number of suicides reduced, and hospitalizations decreased markedly. All this is to the good. One unfortunate result, however, at least from the point of view of psychotherapists, has come about. That is a "devaluation of the psyche." In other words, a whole group of psychiatrists believes that psychiatric illness of all kinds will respond to treatment by impersonal physiological and pharmacological means, and that consequently all attempts at understanding and treatment through psychotherapy or by sociological means are of little or no use.

Behavior Therapy. The devaluation of the psyche has been encouraged by still another historic event. The theory of the conditioned reflex was first put forward by the Russian neurophysiologist Ivan P. Pavlov in the last two decades of the 19th century. His work on dogs was extended to other animals and finally to human beings. So-called "experimental neuroses" were first observed by Pavlov himself in dogs accidentally caught in a flood in his laboratory, and later induced in sensitive animals by bringing about anxiety through conflicting stimuli. In this country a new school of psychology called "Behaviorism" grew up in the early 1900's, and is still flourishing. The treatment of both psychosis and neurosis, it is claimed, can be carried out successfully with little attention to the patients' emotions, fantasies, and thoughts. Instead a method of conditioning and deconditioning is recommended as the only really effective way to relieve symptoms and alter behavior in all functional mental illness, personality disorder and behavior problems.

Diagnosis and Classification. In the preceding paragraphs a number of diagnostic terms have been used. Those naming *organic* disorders are like those used in other branches of medicine. They have gross and microscopic pathology characteristic for each. With the *functional* disorders matters are different. Since there is no typical brain pathology for any of them, their existence depends on *descriptive psychopathology.* This means that they are clinical delineations resting upon cross-section descriptions or mental status examinations, and upon long-section histories of individual cases. The distinctions made by these diagnostic terms consequently correspond to no well-defined clinical entities. They have grown up over the years as aids to thinking and teaching, in accordance with custom and with agreements among members of committees concerned with such matters. Originally each country had its own diagnostic table—the United States among them. In 1968 a table was made which was international. To understand the diagnostic labels for functional mental disorders we must know something of their history.

Pinel had only four diagnostic categories: melancholia, mania (with and without delirium), and dementia, or abolition of the thinking faculty. He was a practical man mainly interested in the institutional management of his patients. The old terms that had come down from antiquity suited him well enough. When the academic psychiatrists began to study patients with scholarly thoroughness, terms began to multiply. In 1860 a French psychiatrist, Morel, introduced the term "demence precoce" (Latinized in German and English speaking countries into "dementia praecox"). Such cases were mostly serious and chronic, beginning in adolescence and early adulthood and progressing to a loss of thinking and adaptive ability analogous to that seen in the very old. Soon further distinctions were made. Hecker gave hebephrenia its name in 1871. Kahlbaum described catatonia in 1874. Not until 1903 did Diem describe dementia simplex. Before that time Emil Kraepelin began including in successive editions of his textbook of psychiatry an increasingly complex system of nomenclature and classification which became standard throughout Europe and America.

Kraepelin. Born in the same year as Sigmund Freud, 1856, Kraepelin (4) studied first with vonGudden, psychiatrist to the mad king of Bavaria, Ludwig the Second. He then worked with Flechsig, at whose sanitarium Schreber (whose case Freud made famous) once stayed, and with Wundt, the pioneer in experimental psychology. The first edition of his textbook appeared in 1883. When a psychological laboratory was built at the University of Heidelberg in 1890 he was asked to head it. There he carried on research on the effects of fatigue, sleep, alcohol, and drugs. Alzheimer joined him there. In 1904 he became director of the first psychiatric research institute in the world, at Munich. It was supported by the Rockefeller Foundation. With all these activities, he continued to study his patients, both in "cross-section" and "long-section," with Teutonic thoroughness. He added to the sub-types of dementia praecox: the paranoid type, differentiating it from paranoia, which was without "dementia," though also primarily delusional. He took part in prolonged and acrimonious controversies over such matters as whether involutional melancholia should be an entity separate from manic-depressive depression. He introduced terms no longer popular, such as "paraphrenia," a condition somewhere between paranoia and paranoid dementia praecox. He died, full of honors, in 1926. By the 1930's progressive young psychiatrists, enamored of dynamic psychiatry, believed him to be a conservative influence whose shackles should be struck off. They had forgotten, or never knew, that Kraepelin had once been a pioneer and leader in psychiatric teaching and research.

Bleuler. In Europe the next important development in classification was the work of Eugen Bleuler (5), professor at Zurich from 1898 to 1939. Born a year after Kraepelin and Freud, in 1857, he studied with Charcot in Paris as well as with vonGudden in Munich. He worked for a short while with August Forel at Zurich. Forel, besides his interests in alcoholism, hypnotism, and sexology, was an authority on the social life of ants. When Bleuler became chief of the Zurich hospital for the chronically insane at Rheinau on the Rhine, he began his work on dementia praecox. A quarter of a century later, in 1911, he finished his great book, *Dementia Praecox, or the Group of Schizophrenias.* In it he broadened the concept of dementia praecox to include acute cases with delusions and hallucinations similar to those in chronic ones, but with a better prognosis and without dementia. He also offered an explanation of its descriptive psychopathology based on association psychology, current in those days. The concept of autism, (withdrawal into a subjective world of fantasy), we owe to him, as well as the idea of ambivalence. He encouraged the younger members of his staff, Carl Jung, Karl Abraham and A. A. Brill among them, to study psychoanalysis. Though in his later years he became disenchanted with analysis, he will always be remembered for his wide-ranging and original mind.

Not translated till 1950, his book enjoyed a second vogue in America. It is still, after 60 years, an authoritative text on schizophrenia.

Meyer. Meanwhile in America, the man who made the greatest contributions to academic psychiatry was another Swiss, Adolf Meyer. He was born near Zurich in 1866, studied with August Forel, and came to the United States in 1892, to teach at the newly formed University of Chicago. To support himself he got a job at the nearby Kankakee State Hospital. There he set up a pathological laboratory and encouraged the doctors to take careful histories from their patients. Whenever he went henceforth, including Worcester State Hospital in Massachusetts, New York State Psychiatric Institute, and Johns Hopkins Medical School in Baltimore, he organized staff conferences, gave lectures and urged the intensive study of each individual patient. He emphasized the evolution of mental illness, beginning in infancy. In 1894 in an article on child study he wrote: "The child of abnormal parents is exposed from birth to acquire unconsciously" morbid habits. After six weeks with Kraepelin at Heidelberg in 1896, he introduced Kraepelin's classification system into America. He married a Radcliffe College graduate in 1902 and soon arranged for her to visit patients' families in their homes. She was a pioneer in psychiatric social work. Though he met Freud and Jung at Clark University in 1909 and was a charter member of the American Psychoanalytical Association, he was never a psychoanalyst himself. At Johns Hopkins in 1914 he organized the first 4-year course in psychiatry for medical students. Colleagues and students became professors of psychiatry and directors of teaching hospitals throughout America and Great Britain.

He was greatly concerned over the conflict between the organic and functional viewpoints. He therefore combined them both in the term "psychobiology." He insisted that man was physicochemical, biological, psychological, and social—all at the same time. He eventually abandoned the Kraepelinian classification, substituting for it at Johns Hopkins his own system of "reaction types." Each psychiatric illness, he said was a biological or psychological reaction to physical or psychological trauma— arising in a person made vulnerable by constitutional, physiological, or historical factors. He called his system "ergasiology," from the Greek word for energy. Unfortunately, his new nomenclature did not catch on. However, his concept of reaction types and his teaching methods became so much a part of American psychiatry that they are pretty much taken for granted. Most mental health workers don't realize that much of our hospital organization and our ways of thinking about patients originated with him. It has been said that wherever he went he transformed asylums into hospitals (6).

Summary. Academic psychiatry added a new dimension to institutional psychiatry. Beginning in the middle of the 19th century its leaders, influenced by the discoveries and theories of pathology, put their major effort first into the study of patients with organic brain disease. They went as far as they could along this avenue with the tools of anatomy and neuropathology that were then available. Their progress, though remarkable, still left unexplained the symptoms of the majority of psychotic patients. They tried to fill in the gap with hypotheses concerning toxins, heredity, and constitution, but could not explain much nor in practice go beyond moral treatment. They even thought they found brain pathology which later neuropathologists could not substantiate, or made elaborate speculations concerning functions of different areas and tracts, called by skeptics "Gehirnmythologie," or neuromythology. Physiological treatments that did meet with some success, in the 20th century, with manic-depressive and schizophrenic disorders, such as fever, insulin, and convulsive therapies, were completely empirical. There were no adequate explanations in terms of neurophysiology of why or how they worked.

The academic men could contribute, as far as the functional psychoses were concerned, only thorough and detailed descriptive psychopathology. This they used as a foundation for elaborate classification schemes, intellectually satisfying but of little practical value to the patients. Much time was wasted on arguments over nomenclature. Scientific objectivity, so valuable and productive in the study of the inanimate and the animal worlds, made little progress in comprehending the aberrations of the human mind. In fact, the devaluation of the psyche that resulted led to a loss of meaningful understanding in terms of emotions and subjective values.

In the early years of the 20th century efforts were being made to break through this impasse, by reviving the subjective world of the psyche without losing the contributions of organicism. It was a Hegelian maneuver on the part of Meyer—the thesis of the organic and the antithesis of the psyche were synthesized in the concept of psychobiology. Still an academic rigidity remained. To break the bonds of intellectual categories and natural science objectivity new observations and new hypotheses were needed, and a new spirit of adventurous inquiry. For such innovations we must return to an underground movement that had been simmering ever since the latter years of the 18th century, beneath the rigid and brittle surface of university psychiatry.

BIBLIOGRAPHY

1. J. G. Spurzheim, *Observations on the Deranged Manifestations of the Mind or Insanity*, Baldwin, Craddock & Joy, London, 1817.

    J. G. Spurzheim, *Phrenology*, Marsh, Capen & Lyon, Boston, 1834 (3rd American Edition)

2. H. J. Dietze & G. E. Voegele, *Wilhelm Griesinger's Contributions to Dynamic Psychiatry*, Dis. of the Nerv. System, 26:579, 1965.

3. S. Weir Mitchell, *The Effects of Anhalonium Lewinii*, British Medical Journal, 2:1625, 1896.

4. Adolph Meyer, *Emil Kraepelin, Obituary*, Amer. J. Psychiatry, 84:749, 1927.

5. A. A. Brill, *Obituary of Eugen Bleuler*, Amer. J. Psychiatry, 96:513, 1939.

6. Alfred Lief, *The Common-sense Psychiatry of Adolf Meyer*, McGraw-Hill, New York, 1948.

Chapter 5

THE BEGINNINGS OF PSYCHOTHERAPY

The Last Exorcist. In 1775 a priest, Johann Gessner, was famous throughout Austria, Bavaria and Switzerland as an exorcist. He said that sickness was of two kinds, natural and preternatural, the latter caused by the devil, sorcery, or demonic possession. When someone was brought before him he entreated the demon to manifest himself. Should the symptoms then appear, he pronounced exorcism; if not, he sent the sufferer to a doctor. Though he relieved the symptoms of many hundreds of men and women, he stirred up opposition among rationalists of the day. One of them was the Prince Elector of Bavaria, Max Joseph. At the Prince Elector's invitation, Franz Anton Mesmer came to Munich to demonstrate his new method of treatment by animal magnetism. On November 24, 1775, before a large and learned audience, he provoked and relieved attacks in an apparent epileptic, without the use of exorcism. Mesmer announced that Father Gessner, though undoubtedly an honest man, was curing patients by magnetism without knowing it. At the Prince's request, the Bishop of Regensburg banished Gessner to a small village. Pope Pius VI directed him to perform the rite of exorcism only with great discretion. Three years later Gessner died (1).

Mesmer. Franz Anton Mesmer was born in 1734 and graduated in medicine at Vienna in 1766. His dissertation was on the influence of planets on human diseases. Marrying a wealthy widow, he was soon a successful practitioner. Among his friends were Leopold Mozart and his precocious son Wolfgang. In 1773 and 1774 he treated successfully a young woman with magnets, according to a method recently discovered in England. He soon concluded that the cure came not from the magnets alone, but also from a magnetic fluid in his own body, which he called "animal magnetism." His patient married Mesmer's stepson. After bringing about several other cures, Mesmer was invited to Munich to controvert Gessner. His Austrian reputation was short-lived. He partially restored the sight of a young blind pianist, whom other physicians had failed to help. These physicians denied the reality of the cure, whereupon the patient relapsed and continued to enjoy her fame as a sightless musician. Soon after, following a period of depression, Mesmer left for Paris.

There he was soon the rage. He had so many patients that he began to treat them in groups. Indoors each patient took hold of a tube placed in a tub of magnetized water. Outdoors less affluent patients touched a magnetized tree. In 1779 he published twenty-seven propositions concerning animal magnetism. Some of them were: that the heavenly bodies influenced men by means of a rarified fluid universally distributed, that this fluid had properties similar to those of a magnet, and it was the vehicle of animal magnetism. By its means physicians could cure nervous diseases directly and other disorders indirectly. Thus, in his words, "the art of healing will reach its final stage of perfection." He organized a society to propagate and practice his doctrines. So much interest and envy were excited by Mesmer's methods and his fees, that in 1784 the king appointed a commission of inquiry. Among its members were the chemist Lavoisier, the physician Guillotin and the American ambassador, Benjamin Franklin. The commission concluded that there was no magnetic fluid and that the phenomena and the cures were produced by imagination. A confidential report to the king indicated the dangers to young women patients from magnetizers stroking their faces and limbs. Some of his disciples rebelled, and Mesmer fled to Switzerland. He died in obscurity in 1812 (2).

Who were the people who went to Gessner and Mesmer? Many of them can be recognized as the hysterics whom we have seen described in the Egyptian papyruses, in the Hippocratean writings and in the Malleus Malificarum. Suggestible, as always, they readily fit themselves into any ritual or technique offered to them. This is not to minimize their suffering. Most of them are unhappy, caught in the conflict between the customs of their society and their emotional needs. In the subsequent years which saw the development of institutional and academic psychiatry, they and their fellow neurotics were largely ignored. They were seldom sick enough to be hospitalized. French academic medicine lost its chance to study and to help them with the decision of the king's commission. So the victims of hysteria and other neuroses struggled on under the care of the general practitioners and the lay therapists of each generation.

Mesmerism, Magnetism and Hypnotism. Mesmer left followers in both France and Germany. They carried on his work outside official medicine, under the name of magnetism. They made further discoveries. In 1787 posthypnotic suggestion was recognized by Lafontain. "Magnetic sleep" or artificial somnambulism—in analogy to sleepwalking—was discovered soon after by a man who was perhaps Mesmer's most remarkable successor, Maxine, Marquis de Puysegur. One of three aristocratic brothers, all interested in mesmerism, he founded a society to train magnetizers, with 200 members by 1789. This Society ended with Puysegur's imprisonment during the Revolution. From 1791 till his death in 1825 he continued his research, treating hundreds of patients. He discovered that many somnambulists could predict the course and duration of their own illnesses. Perhaps the greatest German magnetist was Dr. Justinus Kerner, who lived from 1786 to 1862. He was himself cured of a nervous ailment by magnetism at the age of 12. After earning his medical degree he took up its practice. In 1829 he published a best selling book about one of his patients, whom he called the "Seeress of Prevorst." In France the magnetists continued their efforts to be recognized. In 1825 they submitted a paper to the Academy of Medicine and another commission was appointed, which reported in 1832. The report said that "the results are negative and insufficient in a majority of cases," but that "some results depend solely on magnetism and cannot be produced without it. These are physiological phenomena and well established therapeutically." The report was never printed, perhaps because it was somewhat favorable (3).

In Great Britain, at first, mesmerism fared no better. John Elliotson was Professor of the Practice of Medicine at University College, London. He observed a French mesmerist, Dupotet, conduct a demonstration in 1837. His results, when he tried Dupotet's methods, were so successful that large numbers of students came to observe. When he refused the Dean's request to desist, in 1838 the Council of the college ordered him to cease mesmerizing. Elliotson was the first to use the stethoscope in London, and had already been condemned by several of his seniors for that radical innovation. He resigned all his appointments, and continued his investigations on his own. Besides recording how mesmerism could prevent pain in surgical operations, he asserted how useful it was in treating hysteria. He recognized that hysteria was not necessarily connected with the uterus and occurred frequently in men and boys. He found that children were easy to mesmerize and that their nervous symptoms could often thus be relieved (4). The most remarkable results in surgery were reported about this time by Dr. James Esdaile, a Scotsman working for the East India Company in Calcutta. Beginning in 1845, he performed over 300 major operations under mesmerism, including amputations. Though he was often denounced in medical journals, he persisted until chloroform and ether were introduced about 1850.

We owe to James Braid, another Scottish physician, the term hypnotism. In 1841 he was present at a seance given by the French mesmerist, Lafontain. He at first thought it was all trickery, but soon was convinced that there was something to it. Later in the same year, after experiments on his friends and relatives, he decided that rather than being due to a magnetic fluid, the phenomena were entirely subjective. A clergyman accused him of exercising "Satanic" power. He countered with a physiological theory that by continued monotonous stimulation, the subject suffered from a nervous exhaustion, permitting only the operator's words to occupy his mind. This state he called hypnosis or "nervous sleep." No one but a medical man, he said, was competent to use it. His books were translated into French and German before his death in 1860. He was also an excellent surgeon, specializing in operations for club foot and strabismus.

Still, psychotherapy by means of mesmerism or hypnosis was accepted by very few physicians, especially in institutional or university practice. Three reasons seem to have retarded its use. One was the fear of sexual involvement as we saw in the confidential report to Louis XVI. The second was the aura of charlatanism that hung about Mesmer—his showmanship, exaggerated claims and high fees. This aura (together with his great success among the titled and the wealthy) excited anger, jealousy and envy among conservative medical men. Elliotson, who avoided theatricality and had an excellent reputation as a physician beforehand, ran into the opposition of his conservative elders. A third reason was the air of mystery that surrounded magnetism. Mesmer invoked the power of the planets by way of a universal fluid—resembling the luminiferous ether, respectable among physicists since Isaac Newton. Practitioners used mysterious passes and strokings to induce trances. Justinus Kerner's Seeress, it was alleged, could foretell the future. Elliotson, after he left the University Hospital, experimented with clairvoyance and believed in phrenology. French mesmerists in the 1820's claimed that somnambulists could read with their eyes closed or identify playing cards face down. It was not until the adverse effect of such practices and claims were dispelled by Braid's Scottish common sense and until hypnosis was again taken up in academic circles, that it gained respectability and could have its place among less mysterious forms of treatment.

Charcot: It was in France that acceptance began. The most prominent neurologist in Paris, professor at the Sorbonne, was Jean-Martin Charcot (5). In 1862, at the age of 36, he was appointed chief physician at the Salpêtrière. After prolonged study of hysteria among its patients, he began in 1878 to use hypnotism experimentally. He soon found that they passed through three "stages" of hypnosis: lethargy, catalepsy and somnambulism. In 1882 he read a paper at the Academy of Sciences on his work—the same Academy that had refused a hearing to the magnetists in 1831. In 1884 he demonstrated that many male cases of paralysis following accidents were hysterical. He then produced similar paralyses under hypnosis in subjects who had never been paralyzed nor had hysterical symptoms. In 1892 he distinguished between "dynamic amnesia" in which lost memory could be restored under hypnosis, and organic amnesia, in which memories could not be recovered. For years he gave dramatic demonstrations on Tuesday morning to an audience recruited from all over Western Europe. Sigmund Freud was among them during four months in 1885 and 1886, Charcot was not without critics. Some neurologists deserted him, who had previously admired his pioneer work in syphilis of the central nervous system and in multiple sclerosis, but could not stomach hypnotism. He was accused of being duped by his favorite patients, who were alleged to be trained by interns to perform as their master expected. Catholic clergy denounced him because he replaced nuns by lay nurses. Even the magnetists called him a charlatan. Despite all this, his great and well-deserved reputation as a neurologist made it possible for him and others to conduct clinical and research studies on neurosis and hypnotism in hospitals and university clinics.

Liebault and Bernheim. Meanwhile a general practioner in the French town of Nancy in Lorraine, A. A. Liebault, had for years been quietly practicing the treatment of neurosis by hypnotism. It was not till 1882 that he attracted the attention of Hippolyte Bernheim, professor of internal medicine at the university at Nancy, who on hearing of Charcot's appearance before the Academy of Science, published some of his own and Liebault's work in 1884. In opposition to Charcot, he wrote that hypnotic trance was not an abnormal state, identical with hysterical somnambulism, but the effect only of suggestion in normally susceptible persons. In later years he demonstrated that many effects could just as well be gained with patients who were wide awake. Many physicians came to observe Liebault's and Bernheim's methods, low key and undramatic as they were. Among them were August Forel in 1887 and Sigmund Freud in 1889. Freud translated a book of Bernheim's into German.

At this point our story begins to overlap with the history of psychoanalysis. Other methods than either hypnosis or psychoanalysis were being devised at this time. For example, in 1904 Paul Dubois of Bern, Switzerland, lectured on the "moral treatment" of the neuroses—which he had been using in his sanitarium for some years. It consisted of conscious training of the will (or, as we would say, of the ego) by persuasion and self-education. His approach was empirical, with no theory of how his patients got better. Charcot's work at the Salpêtrière soon lapsed after his death in 1893. Joseph Babinski, he of the reflex, turned against his old master and said that hysteria was merely the result of suggestion. It could be treated, he said, by persuasion alone.

Janet. Charcot's most brilliant student was Pierre Janet. Originally he worked with hysteria, later with obsessive-compulsive neuroses. From 1882 to 1886, while teaching philosophy before going to medical school, he experimented with hypnosis. Combining it with automatic writing, he uncovered a second personality in a hysterical girl. Such double or multiple personalities had been reported at intervals for years. One of the earliest cases, published in 1836 by Antoine Despine, was treated successfully with magnetism. After starting medical school in 1899, Janet contined working with neurotic patients at the Salpêtrière. In subsequent years he developed his own theories and techniques of psychological analysis and synthesis, independent of Freud. The neurotic, he said, suffered from subconscious "fixed ideas" which were at the root of his symptoms and could be reached through dreams, hypnosis, automatic writing or otherwise. Once discovered, the fixed ideas must be synthesized into consciousness by re-education, or else permanently dissociated. The rapport between the patient and the physician had to be handled with great understanding and delicacy.

Except for Janet's work, psychotherapy—hypnotic or otherwise—attracted little attention in academic circles after Charcot's passing. In America, as early as 1880, George M. Beard (6) published, "A Practical Treatise of Nervous Exhaustion (Neurasthenia)," containing excellent descriptions of neuroses, but very little about treatment. S. Wier Mitchell had devised in the 1870's his "rest cure"—keeping patients in bed for weeks while feeding them a heavy diet, in isolation from disturbing relatives (7). Magnetism meanwhile had been taught and practiced in the United States outside medical circles. A young woman named Mary Patterson consulted Phineas P. Quimby, in Portland, Maine, in 1862 (8). Hearing a French mesmerist lecture in Belfast, Maine, in 1838, he soon started his own practice and had been treating people with much success. Mrs. Patterson, unhappily married to a dentist, suffered from weakness, catalepsy and outbursts of temper. After three weeks with Quimby's treatment her symptoms disappeared. Beginning in 1864, she put together some of her own ideas with his, wrote *Science and Health,* and as Mary Baker Eddy, founded Christian Science.

Prince. The practice of hypnotism reached its height in America in the early years of the 20th century. A Boston psychiatrist, Morton Prince, published in 1906 a study of a multiple personality in his book, *The Dissociation of a Personality.* Using every technique to supplement hypnotism he could imagine, including automatic writing, crystal gazing and the administration of ether, he succeeded in uniting his patient's several personalities (9). During the first World War hypnotism was used to treat shell-shock (combat induced hysteria) in the British, and American and German armies. Since he was not welcome at Harvard Medical School, Prince founded the Psychological Clinic at Harvard College, for the study and teaching of psychotherapy. While the practice of hypnosis declined as the influence of psychoanalysis grew, Estabrooks and White continued to work with it at Harvard, with the encouragement of Henry A. Murray.

About the same time at Worcester State Hospital, Milton Erickson began
his ingenious experiments in hypnotic therapy.

Recent Developments. Since Freud found that his patients in Vienna did
not respond to his efforts at hypnosis, he dropped its practice and went on
to invent psychoanalysis. Jung became similarly disillusioned when he found
that a woman he was treating hypnotically contrived symptoms to please
him. Neither Freudians nor Jungians therefore practiced hypnotism. During World War II, combat reactions were treated by intravenous injections
of sodium pentothal rather than by hypnosis. The hypnotic method was not
revived until psychoanalysts discovered that many of their patients reached
plateaus and made no progress for months at a time. To break through this
impasse, some psychoanalysts hypnotized patients with considerable success. Lewis Wolberg (10) of New York dubbed this combined procedure
"hypnoanalysis," At the Menninger Clinic in Topeka, Kansas, a stronghold
of psychoanalysis, Brenman and Gill (11) carried out careful experiments
and clinical trials, followed by a brilliant amalgamation of theories of suggestion and of psychoanalysis. One of the most skillfull of specialists in the
art of hypnosis is Dr. Harold Rosen (12) of Baltimore. Dr. Joseph Wolpe,
the behavior therapist at Temple University School of Medicine, resorts to
hypnosis in some of his more difficult cases.

So this venerable method has returned finally to take its place among
other ways of studying and treating the neuroses. Even though how it
works is still imperfectly understood, there is no doubt as to its usefulness.
Since the discovery of the EEG we know that the hypnotic state is *not*
allied to sleep, since under hypnosis the EEG is like that in the waking state.
We can only say that people who can be hypnotized, whether hysterics or
normals, are more extraverted, more suggestible and more capable of selective concentration. By its means many neurotics can be treated more expeditiously and effectively than without it.

Summary. The treatment of neurosis by psychotherapy began two hundred years ago with the discovery of a mysterious and almost magical way
of releasing symptoms and controlling suggestible patients. At first, progress
was made by exploring the manifold phenomena that could be elicited. A
way had to be found between charlatanism and occultism on the one hand
and fear and skepticism on the other. Concern for the patients' welfare,
scientific caution, and common sense led to recognition of the method's
limitations and to logical application of its benefits. At present, though
still viewed with some doubt, treatment and investigation by methods of
suggestion have their place among other kinds of psychotherapy, whether
they be psychoanalysis, behavior therapy, or simple persuasion and support.

BIBLIOGRAPHY

1. Henri Ellenberger, *The Discovery of the Unconscious*, Basic Books, New York, 1970, p. 53 ff.

2. Robert Darnton, *Mesmerism and the End of the Enlightenment in France*, Schocken, N. Y. 1970.

3. R. E. Shor & M. T. Orne, *The Nature of Hypnosis*, Holt, Rinehart & Winston, New York, 1965, p. 31.

4. J. Milne Bramwell, *Hypnotism*, William Rider & Son, London, 1921.

5. Henri Ellenberger, op. cit., pp. 89 ff.

6. George M. Beard, *Nervous Exhaustion*, William Wood & Co., New York, 1880.

7. S. Weir Mitchell, *Fat & Blood*, Phila., 1877.

8. E. F. Dakin, *Mrs. Eddy*, Scribners, New York, 1929.

9. Morton Prince, *The Dissociation of a Personality*, Longmans Green, New York, 1906.

10. Lewis Wolberg, *Medical Hypnosis*, Grune & Stratton, New York, 1948; *Hypnoanalysis*, Grune & Stratton, N. Y. 1945.

11. Margaret Brenman & Merton M. Gill, *Hypnotherapy*, Internat. U. Press, New York, 1947.

12. Harold Rosen, *Hypnotherapy in Clinical Psychiatry*, Julian Press, New York, 1953.

Chapter **6**

FREUD AND THE NEO-FREUDIANS

Introduction. The history and doctrines of psychoanalysis are very familiar to most students of psychiatry and allied disciplines. So many people have modified those doctrines, or disagreed with them to a greater or less extent, that it is hard to know where to begin. Although Adler and Jung come before many of the Neo-Freudians chronologically, the latter shall be described first, since their concepts are usually closer to Freud's.

The idea of an unconscious mind did not originate with Freud. The need for such a concept goes back to Descartes' distinction, made in the 17th century, between the conscious mind on the one hand and the material world and the body on the other. This sharply defined dualism could not be overcome without a bridge between the two realms, to reestablish the connection between man's conscious awareness and his underlying natural being (1).

Many philosophers wrote of an unconscious mind, in the 18th and 19th centuries, Schopenhauer, Carus and von Hartmann among others. The pioneer psychologist, G. T. Fechner, like Carus, influenced Freud directly. Wilhelm Griesinger, whose phrase, "no mental disease without brain disease" has been quoted previously, wrote in 1867 that "there is in intelligence an actual, though to us an unconscious, life and movement ... A constant activity reigns over this almost, if not wholly, darkened sphere, which is much greater and more characteristic for the individuality than the relatively small number of impressions which pass into a state of consciousness" (2). This sphere is not a mere passive storehouse of memories, such as the psychologist Ebbinghaus demonstrated by testing the recall of nonsense syllables (3), but an active, living state of being. This activity was illustrated by the discovery by the magnetists of post-hypnotic suggestion, and by Charcot of the traumatic origin of hysterical symptoms.

Freud. So the time was ripe, at the end of the 19th century, for Freud's discoveries. Many of the fundamental principles of psychoanalysis were set forth in Breuer and Freud's 1895 book, *Studies in Hysteria,* including repression, conversion, cathexis, sexual trauma and overdetermination. Freud listened to what his patients said, paying close attention to what his predecessors had often considered nonsense. To syndromes which had been only descriptive and static he gave dynamic meaning. He wove a fabric of systematic explanations in terms of the patients' life history. He included dreams, fantasies, symptoms and errors. He indicated a continuous regression from the normal to the abnormal. He offered methods of research and of treatment. Lastly, he wrote well, both dramatically and convincingly. Despite the opposition he stirred up by the theory of infantile sexuality and by his provocative terms, he attracted followers who were nearly as bold and articulate as himself. He was persistent through a period of controversy and neglect, until he was able to establish a school of thought and practice whose originality and utility could not be ignored. He gave the art of psychotherapy an impetus which is still influential.

In 1902 Adler and Stekel and two others began meeting with Freud in the waiting room of his offices at 19 Bergstrasse in Vienna. They were the nucleus of the Vienna Psychoanalytic Society. In the next decade, though Freud got little recognition in his own country, Eugen Bleuler of Switzerland encouraged his students to study Freud's ideas, and G. Stanley Hall of Clark University in Worcester, Massachusetts, invited Freud to lecture there. Freud was delighted with these evidences of academic recognition. "As I stepped onto the platform at Worcester," he wrote, " ... it seemed like the realization of some incredible daydream; psychoanalysis was no longer a product of delusion, it had become a valuable part of reality" (4). In gratitude to Bleuler, Freud nominated his younger colleague, C. G. Jung, to be president of the newly formed International Association for Psychoanalysis.

But this halcyon period did not last. In 1911 disagreements with Adler and Stekel arose, and in 1912 with Jung. Attempts to reconcile their differences failed. By 1913 all three had left the Society. At intervals in later years men and women would become disciples and then leave in the same fashion. A few men were able to disagree deeply with Freud and yet remain on good terms.

The variations in doctrine and practice among these sectarians are so many, and often so subtle, that it is difficult to describe them systematically. One approach is to call them right wing and left wing—right in the sense of taking some principle of Freud's and carrying it to an extreme, left in the sense of disagreeing with respect to several fundamental principles.

Reich. The most evident example of a Freudian "rightist" would be Wilhelm Reich. In his early years as an analyst in Berlin he was struck by the interminable length of many analyses. He concluded that the problem was deeper than that of simple resistance. Rather such patients were confined in "character armor," a very rigid personality structure which made change impossible by ordinary techniques. Consequently, in order to release the dammed up libido, the analyst was forced to break the taboo against touching the patient, and manipulate the limbs or press on the epigastrium in order to penetrate the psychological armor reflected in bodily rigidity. Deciding that free expression of sexual libido was the sine qua non of cure, Reich hypostasized or deified sexuality. Eventually he found it to be one with the energy of the cosmos. After emigrating to the United States, he constructed and sold boxes lined with metal which were intended to reflect this energy back into the body, not only relieving psychiatric illness, but also curing cancer. He was arrested, prosecuted and sent to Federal prison, where he died. Thus a man exiled from his homeland to escape persecution, died in the country which gave him asylum, tragically and prematurely (5, 6).

Klein. A much less extreme example is Melanie Klein, a child analyst who practiced in London, and who never broke with Freud (7). She took Freud's concept of the super-ego, supposed to originate about the age of four, and carried it back to earliest infancy. Consequently, she taught, analysis must reach into the stage of infantile anxiety, aggressiveness, and ambivalence, into the pre-Oedipal period, if it is to be complete. The importance of this period has been buttressed by the work of Rene Spitz on the severe depression suffered by infants abandoned during the first year of life (8). These observations help explain how nearly impossible it is to help psychiatric patients who have been emotionally deprived severely and for prolonged periods in infancy and early childhoood. Melanie Klein, however, was the first to suppose that the "conscience" goes back so far in its origins. The high incidence of sociopathy in graduates of old-fashioned over-crowded and impersonally administered orphanages supports her hypothesis. She recommends, therefore, that infants two years old or less be analyzed, through their fantasy lives as revealed in play, with direct and "deep" interpretation from the start. Her outlook is especially prevalent in Great Britain, with Susan Isaacs, Joan Riviere and D. W. Winnicott among her followers.

Rank. Going back even further into infancy than Melanie Klein, Otto Rank broke with Freud in 1924 with the publication of his book, *The Trauma of Birth.* Rank joined Freud in the Vienna group in 1902, almost at the beginning. He was one of the few early followers of Freud who were not physicians. He became interested in the psychology of artists and in mythology. At the time he came to this country in 1935, he strongly influenced the Philadelphia Child Guidance Center, through Frederick Allen and John Rose, and the University of Pennsylvania School of Social Work and its "functional" school.

Perhaps the most important words in Rank's vocabulary were "relationship" and "separation." The primary relationship was between the mother and child, beginning in the uterus. The first separation (and the first emotional trauma), was birth itself. Ever afterward life was a succession of separations, each necessary, each painful: weaning, going to school, adolescence, marriage, bereavement and, finally, death. The motive force that helped the individual progress from one stage to the next was the will. Will, in Rank's terminology was not just that amount of psychic energy available to the ego, as it has been defined, but rather the source of psychic energy itself. It corresponded to the German philosopher Schopenhauer's concept of will, as portrayed in his book, *The World as Will and Idea:* a cosmic force funneled through each human life.

Rank described four types of people: *the average man,* in whom the will was sublimated through the institutions of his society and channeled into a natural transition from one stage to the next. Second was the *creative or artistic man,* whose will transcended those institutions and brought into being innovations that transformed them. Third was the *antisocial man,* whose will manifested itself impulsively and destructively, rather than creatively, against the institutions of society. Lastly was the *neurotic man* whose will was inhibited so that, unable to overcome his separation anxieties, he continually strove to return to his mother's womb. The neurotic was self-destructive, instead of destructive of society. He could not adapt to society like the average man, nor be creative, except spasmodically.

The treatment of neurotics Rank called "relationship therapy." A creative type, the therapist, encourages the patient to enter into a relationship with him. This relation offers to the patient's faltering ego an illusion of security. The therapist's ego becomes the patient's assistant ego so long as treatment lasts. During the analysis the patient acquires the self-knowledge, energy and courage to include reality rather than exclude it, and so to resume his progress in life and the expression of his will. The first or entering stage of therapy is that of establishing a working relationship, the second is the working phase. In the third or ending phase the patient begins the separation of his ego from that of the therapist with reactivation of all the resistances and anxiety that caused the failure of his previous attempts at separation. If this stage is successful, the patient's ego, no longer self-destructive, becomes constructive. He becomes either an average well-adapted man or his creative capacities are released (9, 10).

Ferenczi. Occupying a place closer to Freud's position, so that they never actually broke with each other, was Sandor Ferenczi. Born in Hungary, he graduated in medicine from the University of Vienna, and met Freud there in 1907. He was at Clark University in Worcester,

Massachusetts, when Freud and Jung were there in 1909. In 1926 and
1927 he lectured at the New School for Social Research in New York. He
died in 1933. He described the "Sunday neurosis"—seen in the man whose
symptoms were quiescent all week while supported by the structure of his
job, but appeared on Sundays and holidays when he had to be with his
family. Ferenczi and Rank experimented with "end setting" in treatment—
another attempted solution to the problem of the interminable analysis.
Ferenczi's most distinctive contribution to psychoanalysis was his emphasis on the need for love. The neurotic typically has been deprived of love
since infancy. The therapist supplies this love, expressing his feelings openly to the patient in order that he can learn to know and express his own
undeveloped capacity for loving. This is the corrective emotional experience. Freud was disturbed by rumors of Ferenczi's unanalytic emotionality in Budapest. If Ferenczi had lived longer a breach might have developed (11, 12).

Horney. One of the first women analysts to be trained in Europe was
Karen Horney, an example of a "left wing" neo-Freudian. Born in Ham-
burg in 1883, she obtained her M. D. at Berlin in 1911. From 1920 to
1922 she was at the Berlin Institute for Psychoanalysis. She wrote papers
on marriage—a subject Freud had had little to say about. Coming to
America in 1932, she was at once struck by the differences between Ger-
manic and American culture. Psychoanalytic theory, she saw, required
modification to be useful in the matriarchal atmosphere of America.
Patterns of neurosis were determined by cultural conditions rather than
by presumed absolutes such as the Oedipus Complex. She traced neurosis
to a "basic anxiety," with secondary maneuvers of submissiveness and
search for personal glory to overcome it. The analyst's task was to help
the patient find his real self, hidden behind the facade of his anxiety and
its disguises. She wrote a series of books, *The Neurotic Personality of Our
Time* and *Neurosis and Human Growth* among them, and founded her
own training institute, the American Institute for Psychoanalysis, before
her death in 1952 (13, 14).

Sullivan. Among the few Americans who made original contributions
to psychoanalytic theory was Harry Stack Sullivan (15). Born in Norwich,
in up-state New York, in 1892, he got his medical degree in 1917, and
died in 1949. For years he carried on research in the psychotherapy of
schizophrenia at the Sheppard and Enoch Pratt Hospital near Baltimore.
Later he became professor of psychiatry at Georgetown University in
Washington, and lectured at the Washington-Baltimore School of Psychoanalysis. He insisted that no personality is an isolated, self-contained entity.

Each of us is part of a complex of interpersonal relationships. The infant begins life in total empathy with its mother, who is its "significant other." Mother and child are in an emotional communion which Sullivan called the "prototaxic" phase—a symbiosis with no division between ego and other, no comprehension of either time or space. As the ego emerges it enters into the "parataxic" phase. Disapproval by significant others—at first of course the parents, causes anxiety to develop in the beginning self-system. Since the schizophrenic self-system is weak it is easier for regression to the parataxic and prototaxic levels to occur.

Fromm. More concerned with social relationships than either Horney or Sullivan is Erich Fromm. He was born in Frankfurt, Germany, in 1900 and earned a Ph. D. in sociology at the University of Munich. Leaving Germany early in the Hitler period, he taught at the New School for Social Research in New York from 1934 to 1939, and since then has been on the faculty of the National University in Mexico City. One of his early books, "Escape from Freedom," was inspired by the realization that democracy in Germany caused much anxiety in men who later welcomed the release from freedom that the Nazi dictatorship offered. Increased self-awareness, individuality and economic and political freedom augmented emotional insecurity. A socialist, he adopted Marx's term "alienation" to describe the depersonalization of the urban masses who so easily became Hitler's followers. Need for love became perverted into symbiotic union with a leader. His followers displayed either the passive masochism of the docile worker, or else the dominating sadism of the storm trooper or the soldier. Mature love, on the other hand, is union with the beloved while preserving the integrity of both. The analyst's task is to transform immature love into mature love, and to help in the creation of social institutions which will replace alienation with genuine social concern and cooperation (16, 17).

Rado. A still different variation on the psychoanalytic theme was composed by another Hungarian, Sandor Rado (18). Coming to New York in the time of Hitler, as did so many able Europeans, he became director of the psychoanalytic training center at Columbia University. Perhaps like Karen Horney under the influence of American practicality, he concluded that the Freudian developmental schema was insufficient, leading as it did to concentration upon the patient's past history. Feeling neglected by his therapist's interest in theory, and wishing to be relieved of his symptoms, the patient rebelled like a defiant child. The therapist, struggling with this resistance, became a reproving parent. Rado got around this contest by "adaptational analysis," a form of emotional reeducation directed at the relief of present suffering in the light of the past. The patient was encouraged to be neither obedient, defiant nor erotically dependent, but a consciously aspiring and developing adult. He strove, with the help of analyst's knowledge and skill, to become self-reliant, progressing rather than regressing. Thus he and his doctor worked together toward personality reconstruction on realistic grounds. One of Rado's students now practicing and writing in New York is Lionel Ovesey. His book, *Homosexuality and Pseudo-homosexuality* (19) is an application of adaptational analysis to the understanding and treatment of homosexuality and paranoia.

Erikson. Eminent among living psychoanalysts is Erik Erikson (20). Of Danish ancestry, he was raised in Germany and originally studied art. While teaching, he became interested in the psychology of childhood and adolescence. He eventually emigrated to the United States. He left California because, well acquainted with totalitarianism, he refused to take a loyalty oath. Though Erikson has strayed considerably from classical psychoanalytic theory, he is still in the fold. Wasn't he analyzed by Anna Freud? In addition, he is a man of great sensitivity and originality. After studying the children of Sioux Indians and citizens of Massachusetts, he became fascinated by the problem of "identity." He supposed that an adolescent has three choices: a positive identity with his culture, a negative identity expressing rebellion against it, or a postponement of identity formation. The first leads to adaptation. The second results in maladjustment in the forms of alcoholism, drug-addiction, homosexuality or some other life-style unacceptable to society. The third results in withdrawal, in the shape of schizophrenia, depression, or the "hippy" scene. From these considerations, Erikson was led to a revision of the scheme of the psychoanalytic oral, anal, and phallic levels. He formulated a series of interlocking stages, beginning with basic trust and mutuality in infancy and ending with a sense of integrity in old age. Growing to the next is the task of each level. The tasks of adolescence are "to maintain the most important ego defenses against the vastly growing intensity of impulses ... to learn to consolidate ... free achievements in line with work opportunity, and to resynthesize all childhood identifications in some unique way, and yet in concordance with the rules offered by some wider section of society." This positive description of the goals of adolescence is preferable to exclusive concern with the pathologies of neurosis, psychosis and behavior disorder. Erik Erikson also became concerned about world peace. A recent book is a study of the life of Mahatma Gandhi.

"There is something blind and boundless in the adventurous schemes of science and technology, which must now be understood in its historical and psychological relation to other modes of conquest and mastery, understood in its individual motivation and in its composite development ... The only alternative to armed competition seems to be the effort to activate in the historical partner what will strengthen him in his development even as it strengthens the actor in his own development—toward a common future identity. Only thus can we ... transcend the dangerous imagery of victory and defeat, of subjugation and exploitation" (21).

A few representative successors to Freud and dissenters from him have been selected in order to illustrate the trends in thought and in treatment in the work of men and women who were stimulated by his genius. Nothing has been said about some very recent schools of psychotherapy—for example, "transactional analysis"—because much of their principles and practice are foreshadowed in those already discussed. More will come out in the presentations of Stekel and Adler, of Jung and of the existential psychiatrists.

BIBLIOGRAPHY

1. L. L. Whyte, *The Unconscious Before Freud*, Basic Books, New York, 1960.

2. H. J. Dietze and G. E. Voegele, *Wilhelm Griesinger's Contributions to Dynamic Psychiatry*, Dis. of the Nerv. System, 26, 579, 1965.

3. Gardner Murphy, *An Historical Introduction to Modern Psychology*, Harcourt Brace, New York, 1929, pp 189 ff.

4. S. Freud, *An Autobiographical Study*, Complete Psychol. Works, Hogarth Press, London, vol. 20.

5. P. A. Robinson, *The Freudian Left*, Harper Colophon, New York, 1969.

6. *The Orgone Energy Accumulator*, Orgone Inst. Press, Rangeley, Maine, 1951.

7. J. A. C. Brown, *Freud & the Post-Freudians*, Penguin Books, London & Baltimore, 1961, pp. 71 ff.

8. Rene Spitz, *Anaclitic Depression, The Psychoanalytic Study of the Child*, Vol. II, Internat. Univ. Press, New York, 1946.

9. Otto Rank, *Will Therapy and Truth & Reality*, Knopf, New York, 1945.

10. Fay B. Karpf, *The Psychology & Psychotherapy of Otto Rank*, Phil. Library, New York, 1953.

11. Izette DeForest, *The Leaven of Love*, Harpers, New York, 1954.

12. Sandor Ferenczi, *Further Contributions to the Theory & Technique of Psychoanalysis*, Hogarth Press, London, 1950.

13. Karen Horney, *The Neurotic Personality of our Time*, Norton, New York, 1936.

14. Karen Horney, *Neurosis & Human Growth*, Norton, New York, 1950.

15. Harry Stack Sullivan, *Conceptions of Modern Psychiatry*, Norton, New York, 1940.

16. Erich Fromm, *Escape from Freedom*, Rinehart, New York, 1941.

17. Erich Fromm, *The Art of Loving*, Harper & Row, New York, 1956.

18. Sandor Rado, *Changing Concepts of Psychoanalytic Medicine*, Grune & Stratton, New York, 1956.

19. Lionel Ovesey, *Homosexuality & Pseudo-homosexuality*, Science House, New York, 1969.

20. Erik H. Erikson, *Identity & the Lifecycle*, Monograph, Psychological Issues, Vol. I, No. 1, Internat. Univ. Press, New York, 1959.

21. Erik H. Erikson, *Insight & Responsibility*, Norton, New York, 1964.

Chapter 7

ADLER AND INDIVIDUAL PSYCHOLOGY

Introduction. In 1902, when Freud formed the nucleus of the Vienna Psychoanalytical Society, two of the four original members were Alfred Adler and Wilhelm Stekel. By 1910 Adler was president of the Society and Stekel vice-president. Both were editors of the psychoanalytic journal, the Zentralblatt. When differences developed between Freud and Adler, Stekel at first maintained that they were reconcilable. After Adler resigned in 1911, Stekel resigned a few months later.

Stekel. First, a little about Wilhelm Stekel. In 1895 he published a paper on coitus among children which came to Freud's notice. Coming to Freud in 1901 for treatment, he was "analyzed" in a few months and became one of Freud's first followers. He was a man of many talents—a pianist, poet and short story writer. Freud admired his unusually intuitive interpretations, but expressed doubts (according to Ernest Jones) of his integrity. After he broke with Freud he published numerous books on the practice of analysis, on the interpretation of dreams, and, above all, on sexual deviations. He criticized the methods of Freud and his followers severely (1, 2). Analyses, he said, were too long and expensive, often resulting in infantilization of the patients. He advised instead an active approach, making three to four months long enough for most analyses. He faced his patient directly with an intuitive estimate of his situation. He recommended the writing down of dreams and the interpretation of manifest content from a minimum of associations, considering the prospective and prognostic significance, with reference to the future as well as the past. He maintained that in criminals and deviates the super-ego was repressed rather than absent. Despite all these differences he continued to call himself a psychoanalyst.

Adler. Adler by 1912 had started his own school which he called *Individual Psychology.* Its roots go back to a publication of his in 1907 concerning "organ inferiority." In many children one organ is constitutionally defective. The body reacts to this defect by compensation, either within the organ itself or in a corresponding one. If one kidney is damaged the opposite one enlarges, or another part of the body will make up for the deficiency—a child with crippled legs will develop strong arms. There can also be "psychological compensation"—a boy with a weak body will strive to become an athlete, a man with poor hearing will study music (like

Beethoven) or with defective vision will become an artist (like El Greco). When Adler spoke at Harvard in the 1930's a student asked him in the question period if a psychiatrist is compensating for a weak mind. Adler countered: "I see that my friend is a psychologist."

In his first book after he went on his own (3), Adler spoke of the inferiority feeling appearing in a child who compares himself to his bigger and stronger father, mother, or older sibling. From this observation Adler derived his psychology of the family constellation (4). The child is forced from birth, at least in Western Europe, into a competitive attitude. The oldest child, feeling inferior to his parents, especially (in a patriarchal society) to his father, attempts to compete with them. He has the advantage over his younger siblings of being the only child at first, and then the biggest one. He may gain from being the favorite, or he may feel dethroned when his mother perforce pays more attention to the second child. While the oldest is often the father's favorite, the second is usually the mother's child. If he is a boy, the second may choose a career opposite to the father's, while the eldest is most likely to follow in his father's footsteps. To make up for his position in his brother's shadow, the second may try to excel either by being well-behaved or else by being rebellious or original. The last born is never dethroned and consequently may be spoiled by his mother's undivided attention. The only-child also may be indulged because he never has to compete with a sibling. In relation to his contemporaries outside the home the only-child may seek a sheltered position, or feel more at home with adults. We see father's girls and mother's boys as examples of favorites, with invidious comparisons of the less-favored, who may be less bright or unattractive. These last, along with those who are pampered or raised too strictly, may be predisposed to neurosis. Normal children have the same stresses to a lesser degree, with less inclination toward over-compensation.

Sexual inequality causes further complications. The boy dreads being thought effeminate and consequently goes out of his way to prove his masculinity. The girl protests her feminine role, especially if she has younger brothers. If there is any implication that a boy's sexual organs are small, a particularly damaging feeling of inferiority arises. A 17 year old boy, after several suicide attempts since the age of 7, finally nearly succeeded in killing himself. It was months before he could tell that since childhood he had believed his penis to be too small and that he consequently felt most inferior both with respect to other boys and in his capacity some day to satisfy a woman. The man equates being above the woman in sex relations with being superior; the woman considers being below as submission. A dominant woman wants to take the top position, literally or figuratively. The Oedipus theme Adler explained as primarily a need to surpass the father and secondarily the directing of his wishful impulses toward his less threatening mother.

Adler's point of view has two philosophical antecedents. The first is Friedrich Nietzsche's "will to power," the second, Hans Vaihinger's *Philosophy of As If."* Vaihinger's book of that name appeared in 1911. In his early years Adler said, the child creates a "guiding fiction"—how his life would be "as if" his fantasy of his future were to come about. This helps to set his "life style"—of dominance or submission or of passive-aggressive behavior. Whatever conflicts with this fiction is repressed. The earliest memory often indicates the life style and the theme of the guiding fiction.

The neurotic character interprets every situation in terms of competition. In Adler's phrase, "every contact is a contest," in which he can be either demanding and assertive, or else fawning and submissive.

There are several principles underlying Adler's work. The first is that aggression, sparked by the will to power, is the primary expression of psychic energy. Sexual behavior is interpreted in terms of aggression and competition, rather than the other way round. The second is the importance of the individual. While Freud emphasized the attraction of the ego toward the object, Adler accentuates the barriers between the individual and the object, hence his name for his school: "Individual Psychology." The third is the importance of the future, or the teleological outlook, as opposed to Freud's dwelling on the past. The individual is always striving toward the realization of the goal set by his guiding fiction (corresponding to Horney's "quest for glory"). If an active person, he tries to shape his environment toward his goal, rather than passively adapting to it. In middle life he may begin to realize he can never reach his goal, thus bringing on either depression or (less often) paranoia.

Adler makes little reference to the unconscious mind. He speaks of the repression of whatever conflicts with the guiding fiction. Infantile feelings of inferiority are forgotten. Egoism, envy and greed are frequently unconscious. Dreams may strengthen the guiding fiction, searching for solutions that will preserve it against the stress of immediate problems. Dreams may point toward the future. They are graphic rehearsals of the attitudes we shall adopt on waking, much as children's play anticipates adult roles. His psychology is concerned mostly with the ego. He anticipated much that Freud wrote in the 1920's when he turned his attention to the ego, and that Freudians have written since. Freud recognized Adler's contributions to ego psychology. He feared that once concerned with the ego analysts would forget the more important unconscious level of the mind. This has actually happened in recent years among many psychotherapists.

What were Adler's solutions to the problems which he raised? Psychotherapy as he taught it was largely reeducation. Logically enough, he decided that the treatment of children was most important. He began child guidance clinics in the Vienna School system in 1919 and continued them till the Nazi occupation in 1934. He had individual psychology taught to teachers so that they could correct the mistakes of parents. He did not use play therapy. He approached children in a simple, rational and matter-of-fact way, with little emotionality. They were treated with respect, as persons of importance. Equality was the basis of treatment, forestalling resistances. The child was shown the conditions with which he was contending, their meaning and how to establish fresh bases of contact with those at home and in school. Ideally, education should begin in the first 5 years, before the life style sets. There should be security in the beginning, then a home atmosphere of consistency, firmness and flexibility. The aim was training the child toward independence. Spontaneous play was important in learning team-work and cooperation.

Beginning with a criticism of family life as a source of pathology and the origin of neurotic character weakness, Adler went on in later years to sketch future ideals toward which the family and society as a whole should grow, in other words, his own guiding fiction, his own teleological goal. He made a good start toward its realization in the child guidance centers he helped to found. Their fruition was interrupted by the Nazi occupation. He escaped, like so many of his contemporaries, to the United States. Arriving in New York in 1930, he taught at Long Island University, now part of the State University of New York. Adler lectured at Harvard and elsewhere in this country and abroad. He died in Scotland in 1937 while on a lecture tour there.

In 1948 the Alfred Adler Consultation Center and Mental Hygiene Clinic was opened in New York City, with Adler's son Kurt as supervising psychiatrist. He is also Medical Director of the Jamaica Center of Psychotherapy on Long Island. A volume published in 1959 (5), in commemoration of the 10th anniversary of the Adler Center, tells us about the treatment of patients by Adlerian methods in recent years.

A Case Example. Here, for example, is a case of "transvestitism": a man in his early thirties, married, with apparent normal sex relationship with his wife. Since early childhood he had fantasies of wearing women's clothing and masturbated. After four years of marriage his wife found out about it and suggested he see a psychiatrist. His early history was typical of this sort of case. When he found a fur collar of his mother's as a child, his mother let him wear it. Soon after when an aunt gave his mother some girl's clothing his mother put it on him and said he looked like a pretty girl. He was the oldest of three children, his brother and sister being twins four years younger. His brother was strong and a fighter, while the patient was frail and had poor eyesight. His mother was domineering, his father a lenient man who lost one job after another. His mother made all the decisions. When the patient grew up he relied on others to make his decisions.

He could not assert himself at work nor with his friends. Except for his poor vision (for which he refused to wear glasses) he was physically well, and his intelligence was above average. Psychological tests showed him to be anxious, obsessive-compulsive, and slightly depressed.

A goal of reconstruction was decided upon for therapy—to help him develop his intellectual and personality qualifications, to raise his self-esteem and to apply his abilities to a more realistic concept of life. He was seen individually once a week. He was considered to be a classical case of "masculine protest"—inferiority feelings with respect to masculinity based on a distorted concept of the role of the male: shunning responsibilities, fearing women by copying them. He felt sorry for himself and believed women were better off: "Nobody expects so much of them." His wife was invited in, found to be mature and willing to help. She was found to be pregnant and would soon have to stop working. This disturbed the patient because of the additional responsibility laid upon him. During three months of treatment he became better able to speak up for himself on the job and with people in general. He appreciated his wife's efforts to help him and became more affectionate with her. Once she suggested that he put on women's underwear while she put on his and then that they would look at each other in a mirror. Unexpectedly he then found that he did not like himself at all as a woman and felt greatly relieved. Soon after he decided he was better and terminated treatment. Follow up six months later found that they had a baby boy. He was concentrating on his future and his work, no longer bothered by his compulsion. There was one problem—he was bossy and didn't want to help his wife at home—"a woman's job," as though he were expected to be a housewife. They were counseled on becoming both individually independent and mutually dependent wherever appropriate.

Social Interest. In his later years Adler became more and more concerned with the reform of society. For the over-emphasis on competition of present-day society he would substitute cooperation founded upon community feeling. An individual with community feeling puts the welfare of society above his own welfare; self-interest is replaced by social interest. In this light the feeling of superiority could become more than merely compensatory for the feeling of inferiority. Community feeling channels the feeling of superiority into achievement in the interests of society; what R. White calls "competence." This is the Adlerian version of "sublimation." Learning occurs not only under the stress of anxiety, but also as a function of curiosity, of interest in the environment and of growing satisfaction in one's ability to adapt to it and change it. As competence grows so do self-esteem and confidence. Another strong base is laid for a genuine feeling of superiority, apart from what others think.

Summary. Stekel can be considered the founder of brief psychotherapy, using psychoanalytic insights in an intuitive and directive fashion. Adler was the originator of ego psychology and of psychotherapy aimed at growth in ego-awareness and ego strength. He was not the only psychiatrist working along these lines. Paul Dubois in Switzerland had used his persuasive approach in the early 1900's. In Massachusetts Austen Riggs soon after developed similar methods at his sanitarium in Stockbridge.

In the 1920's Freud finally turned his attention to ego psychology, followed by his daughter Anna, Paul Federn and others. It was theorized that the ego had libido of its own, apart from that available to the id and super-ego. In the past few years Eric Berne and his followers have been writing about Transactional Analysis. Berne's book, *Games People Play* is almost purely Adlerian, but one looks in vain among the bibliographical references for Adler's name. Harris, in his book, *I'm OK, You're OK* does refer briefly to him. Albert Ellis and Rollo May owe much to Adler in their theories and methods. Like the transactional analysts, they have made original contributions as well. William Glasser's reality therapy relies heavily on Adlerian principles. Even a behavior therapist like Joseph Wolpe, in so far as he encourages assertiveness, is an Adlerian in disguise.

In the words of Joseph Wilder: "Adler's Individual Psychology with its stress on social and ego psychology never met with serious opposition except from the Freudian school. Its findings were quietly and readily absorbed like rain by the thirsty summer earth. They seemed so obvious, penetrated so easily into the minds of practicing psychotherapists, educators, teachers, social workers, parents, and writers that many of them soon honestly believed that these ideas were their own." As Robert W. White wrote: "We have learned to observe the subtle operation of strivings for power, the purposive and aggressive elements in neurotic symptoms, the jealousy and inferiorities and compensations that result from competition and sibling rivalry, the poisoning of social feeling by needs for self-enhancement, and the gradual release of social interest as the patient moves in the direction of health. Fifty years ago these things were never reported and may not even have been perceived ... yet we accept them as nothing more than clinical common sense" (5).

BIBLIOGRAPHY

1. Wilhelm Stekel, *Techniques of Analytical Psychotherapy*, W. W. Norton, New York, 1940.

2. Wilhelm Stekel, *The Interpretation of Dreams*, 2 vols. edited by Emil Gutheil, Liveright, New York, 1943.

3. Alfred Adler, *The Neurotic Constitution*, Dodd Mead, New York, 1930 (introduction dated 1912).

4. Lewis Way, *Adler's Place in Psychology*, George Allen & Unwin, London, 1950.

5. *Essays in Individual Psychology*, edited by K. A. Adler & D. Deutsch, Grove Press, New York, 1959.

Chapter 8

JUNG AND ANALYTICAL PSYCHOLOGY

Introduction. In 1907 a psychiatrist from Zurich came to see Sigmund Freud. Freud had heard that Eugen Bleuler was encouraging the study of his work, and that Carl G. Jung, Bleuler's assistant, had been investigating unconscious complexes by means of an association experiment. Pleased at finally being recognized in an academic center, and at this experimental confirmation of his clinical observations and theories, Freud invited Jung to Vienna.

Carl Gustav Jung's grandfather (of the same name) had been professor of medicine and of anatomy at the University of Basel. His own father was a clergyman. Jung had decided to follow his grandfather's profession, and (after reading Krafft-Ebing's text-book) to become a psychiatrist. In his medical thesis (1) on the case of a hysterical medium, he had cited Freud's *Interpretation of Dreams.* He then embarked on his association experiments at Burghölzli, based on observations made in the 1880s by the pioneer English psychologist, Francis Galton (2). Jung made a list of 100 common words, to which he asked patients and normals to give the first word that came into their minds. He noted the response, timed it with a stop-watch, and observed any other manifestations that occurred. Unusual words, repetitions, prolonged or emotional responses were considered to be *"complex* indicators." Later he combined the test with the psychogalvanometer (the basis for the "lie detector"). He then turned his attention to the study of schizophrenia, or "dementia praecox," as it was then called. He published a monograph, *The Psychology of Dementia Praecox (3),* combining the results of clinical observations and the association test. In his *History of the Psychoanalytic Movement* Freud wrote: "The Zurich group became ... the nucleus of the little band who were fighting for the recognition of analysis. ...The association experiments ... had been interpreted by them in a psychoanalytic sense. ... By this means it had been possible to arrive at rapid experimental confirmation of psychoanalytic observations" (3).

For the next 5 or 6 years Jung considered himself a disciple of Freud's. He was an editor, with Freud and Bleuler, of the *Yearbook for Psychoanalytical and Psychopathological Research.* He became first president of the International Psychoanalytical Association, and published several papers on psychoanalysis. Freud even considered transferring to Jung the leadership of the movement (4, p. 329).

In 1912, however, dissension began. In the afore-mentioned Yearbook, Jung published a monograph, *Transformations and Symbols of the Libido* (5), discarding the concept of sexual libido for that of psychic energy in general. Later, Jung wrote: "I knew in advance that its publication would cost me my friendship with Freud" (6). In 1913, after fruitless efforts to work out their differences, they parted and never met again. While Switzerland was isolated from Austria during the first World War, Jung continued to develop his ideas.

Ego psychology. His ego psychology was influenced by his observations of the disagreement between Freud and Adler. As he saw it: "With Adler the emphasis is placed on a subject ... who seeks his own security and supremacy; with Freud the emphasis is placed wholly upon objects, which ... either promote or hinder the subject's desire for pleasure. This difference can hardly be anything else but a difference of temperament, a contrast between two types of human mentality. ... The spectacle of this dilemma made me ponder the question: are there at least two different human types, one of them more interested in the object, the other interested in himself?" (7)

Psychological Types. These two types arose from a preponderance of one of two attitudes, the "extraverted" or the "introverted." These terms have become so much part of popular language that most have forgotten that Jung introduced them. The man who is primarily extraverted is most interested in people and objects in the outer world, while the primarily introverted person is mostly concerned with the inner world of feelings, fantasies, and ideas. It is not true that all humanity can be sharply divided into two groups of extraverts and introverts. Both attitudes exist in everyone, in accordance with the curve of normal distribution. Among neurotics, extraversion inclines one toward hysteria and introversion toward obsessive-compulsive symptoms. Among psychotics, one will be susceptible to manic-depressive illness, the other to schizophrenia. H. J. Eysenck believes he has confirmed these relationships by factor analysis (8).

In addition, as he wrote in his book *Psychological Types* (9), Jung described four psychological functions: sensation, intuition, feeling, and thinking. Through the sensation and intuition functions we receive information from the external and the internal worlds. Sensation is more detailed and analytical, while intuition operates in terms of wholes. For example, when a patient walks into a psychiatrist's office, the physician observes the patient's dress, expressions, gestures, tone of voice, and so on. At the same time he gains a general impression to which he responds intuitively, often unconsciously. A good psychiatrist is as aware of his intuitions as he is of

details that come through his senses. On the introverted side, he should be
equally aware of his feelings, fantasies, and ideas, though this will be easier
for the more introspective. It is with the feeling and thinking functions
that we classify and evaluate the data from the first two. For this reason
sensation and intuition are called the "non-rational" functions, while the
others are called "rational." When we categorize people, things, or ideas
in accordance with intellectual formulas of rightness or accuracy in terms
of science, mechanics or our standards of behavior, we are using our *thinking function.* When we evaluate them with regard to our feelings toward
them—whether we like or dislike them, or consider them ugly or beauti-
ful by aesthetic standards, or (for that matter) are indifferent to them—
we are exercising our *feeling function.* Highly educated people, in America,
at least, are not used to considering feeling judgments to be rational, but a
music or a drama critic certainly makes use of his emotional responses to
a symphony or a play while judging it.

Jung came to the conclusion that there are eight fundamental kinds of
people: extraverted sensation, intuition, feeling, and thinking, and four
corresponding introverted types. As a child grows he differentiates into
one of these types in accordance with his inborn temperament, modified
by his familial or cultural environment. It has been observed in the nurser-
ies of maternity hospitals that some infants are more active than others.
The active ones are presumably the future extraverts; the quieter ones, the
potential introverts. That function with whose exercise the child is more
skillful or which he feels more sure of, will differentiate more because it is
used more. At the same time we are influenced by what is expected by
those around us. A salesman will expect his children to be more extraverted and intuitive; a scholar will want his to be more introverted and thought-
ful. Our American culture is more extraverted than that of India. The culture of North Germany is oriented toward thinking, that of Bavaria toward
feeling. If a child's natural bent is in accordance with his family's and society's expectations, he will find differentiation easy, but if it is different,
then there may be conflict and maladjustment. Another source of conflict
is the fact that sensation and intuition are opposites, and so are feeling and
thinking. In other words, to use the sensation function well, intuition must
remain unconscious, and vice versa; likewise with feeling and thinking. A
thinking type, for example, will often be subject to outbursts of anger
which he can't explain or will rationalize afterward, saying "I was not myself." Of course his anger is part of himself; his thinking ego just doesn't
admit it. The function which is best developed is called the "superior
function," that next most differentiated the "auxiliary function," and
that least, the "inferior"—opposite, of course, to the superior one. The
superior and an auxiliary function may shift places during a lifetime, just

as one may become more extraverted or introverted in middle or later life, but the inferior function almost never becomes superior.

Persona and Shadow. Another aspect of Jung's psychology of the ego is the separation of the "persona" from the "shadow." The persona is that part of the ego which mediates between the subject and the outer world. It is an amalgam of the most developed attitude and function. The name is derived from that of the masks worn by classical actors. Two of them, those of comedy and tragedy, we often see on the front of theater programs. Through it the ego adapts to external reality—interacting with it and protecting itself from it. The more extraverted emphasize interaction, the introverted protection. At the same time the persona represses those impulses, feelings and images which are unacceptable to one's parents and to society. They then become unconscious complexes, capable of interfering, when repression falters, with the efficiency of the persona. I like to compare the persona to a Venetian blind. When a person wishes to act in the outer world, or communicate with it, he leaves the blind open, but when he wishes to protect himself from that world, either because it is threatening or because he wishes to contemplate his inner world, he pulls the cord and closes the slats. Some have poorly developed personas. They can neither adapt to external reality, nor shield themselves from it. Some people have an inflated persona, with little behind it, like the doctor who is all bed-side manner or the hostess who is overly effusive. In a young person the aim of psychotherapy is often to develop an adequate persona. In an older patient the purpose may be to get behind a too rigid persona to learn about the less developed functions and the deeper levels of the mind.

These deeper levels Jung called the "personal" and the "impersonal" unconscious—the latter better known as the "collective" unconscious. The personal unconscious, which Freud discovered, is the shadow, the door to the collective. In dreams and fantasies the shadow is represented by figures of the same sex as the dreamer, who appear in some way disreputable or criminal. In nightmares, when such figures are threatening, the meaning is that the patient has a problem in his present day life which he is not facing or cannot solve. An example would be a dream of a young man that he was being chased down a dark street by criminals, who were shooting at him. Seeing a brightly lit store, he dodged inside and hid behind a counter. The criminals went running by. An interpretation is that the young man had problems handling his own and others' aggressiveness, and so repressed it and took refuge in conscious activity. The shadow may show itself in impulses or emotions, such as temper-outbursts, of which the persona is ashamed, and apologizes for. The unacceptable behavior or feeling does come from within him, but is not part of what his persona wants to consider to be his true self.

The Collective Unconscious. The theory for which Jung is best known concerns the "collective unconscious." This is the archaic level, presumably inherent, which corresponds in the mind to the reflexes and the instincts or drives in the lower levels of the nervous system. Where complexes in the personal unconscious were once in consciousness or close to its threshold, collective images have never come close to the surface and therefore were never repressed. They are shared by all members of the human race, though the way they express themselves may be partially determined by the culture.

Archetypal Images. Just as motor reactions are mediated through reflexes, so the collective unconscious shows itself through archetypal images. These images are archaic and primordial, recurring throughout art, legends, fairy tales, and religious symbolism. Jung identified them while reading ethnology and comparative religion, in an attempt to understand the bizarre productions of his schizophrenic patients. The archetypal images occur in two chief forms: archetypal situations on the one hand and personifications and symbols on the other. They may be seen as symptoms, in dreams and fantasies, or as projections or identifications.

Perhaps the easiest way to explain the geography of the collective unconscious is through dream images, since nearly all of us have them. The persona and shadow are archetypal images of a sort, though conscious or close to the surface. The first of the collective images that is usually encountered in treatment is that representing the contrasexual inclinations —called the "anima" in the male, and the "animus" in the female, from the Latin word for soul. If a young man dreams of a young woman who is attractive, perhaps seductive, whom he does not know or is only slightly acquainted with, in romantic surroundings, he is dreaming of an anima image. A similar dream image for a young woman would be male. When the anima or animus is projected, the result is falling in love, characteristically an overwhelming, irrational event, accompanied by strong idealization. If, however, a young man projects his anima on his mother (or a girl her animus on her father) a fixation may occur, accompanied by identification with the projected image. The result may be homosexuality, bisexuality, or transsexuality. In adults, the anima and animus may express themselves in creative activity, through art or music, more often than not without homosexual trends. It is no accident that in Ancient Greece the muses were female, since creativity was encouraged only in men. Perhaps Sappho had a male muse!

A young man of 15 or 20 may dream of an adventurous man in a setting of ancient or medieval times. This would be an example of the archetypal image of the Hero. For instance, a college student was once referred to me with depression following the realization that he was in love with a male classmate. His mother had treated him like a girl when he was little, while his father, a busy professional man, was seldom home and had since died. Early in treatment the patient had a dream of a medieval castle, with the drawbridge up, the portcullis down and no one visible on the battlements. On a field between the patient and the moat was a stallion trying to mate with a mare. This dream portrayed the lack of heroic expression in a young man identified with his mother, having a poor father-image, and in whom sex was felt to be animal-like. However, a hero image is implied in the stallion—presumably belonging to a knight within the castle. In later dreams the patient talked with a racing driver—a common adolescent hero-figure—and saw his father closer to him than he had been in his lifetime. The hero image may be projected upon athletes or military men or political figures. A man of ability may attempt to embody the hero image himself. Our patient, for example, majored in English with a writing career in mind. When last seen he had established better relations with women and was well started on his career as a radio and television writer. Since our culture makes little room for heroic women, the hero image is usually fused with the animus in women, and projected on a man. Some women can break with this patriarchal stereotype and become successful in a profession.

Next we come to the image of an older man or woman, called the "Old Wise Man" or "Great Mother" figure. As an example I use a dream of my own. I visualized myself visiting a kindergarten whose attractive teacher (my anima) was showing me how she taught geography. She pointed out a row of small chairs with the name of a country on each. A child would be asked to choose a chair and then tell about that country. Going along with it, I sat in a chair marked Ireland. At once I found myself in Ireland, in a Protestant church! Three other men and I were engaged in taking up the collection. When we went to the front of the congregation with our plates I found that mine had much less in it than did the others'. I immediately thought: "Brother Benedict has been helping himself from the collection again." Stepping outside, I found an elderly monk standing in a garden. I asked him if he had been taking collection money. With a twinkle in his wise eyes he said: "Yes, I needed for my thyme." As you can imagine, this gave me and my analyst food for several weeks' discussion. The dream indicated that it was about "time" that I paid attention to an older wisdom than that of my Protestant ancestors. Besides introducing an old wise man, this dream illustrates how the anima image can put the dreamer in contact with other archetypal images.

The Great Mother image, described masterfully by Erich Neumann (10), may manifest itself in a religious figure, such as the Virgin Mary or the goddess Diana. She may be embodied in a domestic matriarch or a feminine leader, for example, Mary Baker Eddy, called Mother Eddy by Christian Scientists. In the abstract, an example is the "Nature" of 19th century scientists, always spoken of as feminine.

Each of these personifications has its negative aspect too. The anima may appear as a destructive woman, like the young witch in Goethe's Faust from whose mouth crawled a lizard, or the "femme fatale" who leads men to suicide and insanity. The hero may be a demagogue, such as Adolph Hitler. The sage may be portrayed as a mad scientist, bent on destroying the world. The Great Mother appears in the Hindu goddess, Kali (in her negative role), with a necklace of skulls and a river of blood flowing from her mouth. Even God has his Devil and Christ his Antichrist.

In its positive aspect the divine figure represents the Self—the ultimate harmonizing archetype, inclusive of the totality of both consciousness and the unconscious, personal and collective. The Self may also be symbolized by a king or queen, or geometrically by a square or a circle. Jung wrote of the mandala—a Buddhist meditation painting-the cross and the yang-yin symbol as Self symbols.

The situational archetypal images appear in settings standing for transitions from one stage in life to another. The Oedipal situation was the one which Freud discovered and became so fascinated by that he believed it to be the most important of all. Adolescence, the menopause, and death all have their transitional and initiatory images—crossing bridges, going over mountain passes, rites of entry and departure (11), and the like.

Treatment. How can these concepts be used in the understanding and treatment of personality and psychiatric problems? I have said how lack of persona development, irruptions of shadow-material, and type conflicts can lead to symptoms and to complex formation. When evaluating a case, or in the course of treatment, it may be evident that the patient's natural type (attitudinal or functional) is different from the one on the surface. The patient may be conforming to what is expected by his family or his culture. The Myers-Briggs Type Indicator test is useful for identifying type development (12). Once identified, type orientation can be gradually changed through the patient's insight and encouraging a break with the old ways while new ways are fostered and trained.

Marital problems can often be understood and helped by combining type determination with the identification of shadow and anima-animus conflicts. Opposites frequently marry. Originally attracted by their differences, each hopes the other will complement his or her strengths and weaknesses. What was at first attracting becomes after marriage a source of conflict. In our culture a frequent combination is the thinking-sensation man who marries a feeling-intuitive woman, one extraverted and the other introverted. The wife most often asks for help, saying that her husband is unfeeling while he claims that she is too emotional and illogical. An example was a woman in her early 30's with two small children, married to an engineer. She was considering divorce. When she would ask him, with considerable emotion, to take more part in family life, he would retreat to the cellar, where he had a short-wave set, and talk to someone in Australia. The contrast in their personality types was obvious. She appeared to be extraverted, with the feeling function predominant, while he was an introverted thinking type. I scheduled alternating individual and couple interviews—first with her, then with him, then both together. After a few months they were able to comprehend what was going on and change their behavior accordingly. The marriage was going much better when they were last seen.

In the course of similar marriage conflicts the anima and animus may be involved. When a young man and a young woman project upon each other these images, they fall in love. If subsequent disharmony, because of type clashes, causes dissatisfaction, the projection may be withdrawn, by one or both partners. A new projection is then ripe to fall upon another man or woman. An extramarital affair may result. If a strong superego precludes infidelity, unconscious projection may focus on a son or daughter, or on an outsider who embodies the masculine or feminine ideal—perhaps a physician or a clergyman, or some other "charismatic" person. A creative young man may find a "femme inspiratrice" outside his marriage. Treatment consists in developing insight regarding both the personality clashes and the projections, working toward a more mature reestablishment of love within the marriage. Since the anima and animus also carry much creative energy, their expression in artistic or literary work helps those who have talent.

Artists and writers and people with religious interests often find the Jungian approach more congenial than the Freudian. The Jungian therapist recognizes the archetypal images that such patients often experience spontaneously and makes use of them in treatment. In recent years many young people have become acquainted with the archetypal world through psychedelics (13). Frightened or fascinated by their visions, they search for understanding. Often they find it in Jung's books or in the Jungian therapist's office. In adolescence or early adulthood archetypal images may force their way into consciousness, precipitating an acute schizophrenic attack. Jung's theories can often be applied in the psychotherapy of such cases. Many men and women, in the 35 to 40 year age period sought Jung out because of depressions occurring despite outward success. He was able to help them by encouraging them to explore their inner worlds. When they became aware of the images which were clamoring for expression but could not penetrate the ego-defenses, a broader and more harmonious development of personality began. This process may be facilitated by means of "active imagination"—the stimulation of conscious fantasies, beginning perhaps with a dream, in which archetypal images appear. In this way the patient may continue his own individuation after formal analysis or psychotherapy ends. Such constructive fantasy may lead to artistic or literary creation.

Summary. In general it may fairly be said that Jung's approach makes good use of the positive and healing potentialities of the deeper levels of the unconscious, without ignoring the negative and destructive aspects of the collective unconscious. The healing aspect shows itself in savior and rebirth images, so common in religious experience.

BIBLIOGRAPHY

1. C. G. Jung, *On the Psychology of So-Called Occult Phenomena,* 1902, Collected Works. Vol. l, p. 69, Pantheon Books, N. Y. 1957.

2. Gardner Murphy, *An Historical Introduction to Modern Psychology,* Harcourt Brace, New York, 1929, p. 168.

3. *The Psychology of Dementia Praecox,* 1907, Collected Works, vol. 2, p. l, Pantheon Books, N. Y. 1960.

4. S. Freud, *Jahrbuch der Psychoanalyse,* 1914; Coll. Papers, Hogarth Press, London, 1950, Vol. 1.

5. C. G. Jung, *Symbols of Transformation,* Collected Works, Vol. 4, Pantheon, N. Y., 1956.

6. C. G. Jung, *Memories, Dreams, Reflections,* Pantheon, N. Y., 1963, p. 167.

7. C. G. Jung, *Two Essays on Analytical Psychology,* Collected Works, Vol. 7, Pantheon, N. Y., 1953, p. 42.

8. H. J. Eysenck, *The Structure of Human Personality,* John Wiley, New York, 1953, p. 25.

9. C. G. Jung, *Collected Works,* Vol. 6, Princeton U. Press, 1971.

10. E. Neumann, *The Great Mother, an Analysis of the Archetype,* Pantheon Books, New York, 1955.

11. Joseph L. Henderson, *Thresholds of Initiation,* Wesleyan U. Press, Middletown, Conn. 1967.

12. Isabel B. Myers, *Educational Testing Service,* Princeton, N. J., 1962.

13. R. E. L. Masters and Jean Houston, *The Varieties of Psychedlic Experience,* Dell, New York, 1966.

Chapter 9

EXISTENTIAL PSYCHIATRY

If the organicists have taken care of the body, Freud the personal unconscious, Jung the archaic unconscious, Adler, Anna Freud and Neo-Freudians the ego and society, what is there left to investigate? When seeking to be an innovator, it is wise to question the premises upon which contemporary theories and practice rest. To put it another way, one should consider the philosophical groundwork. This is exactly what "existential psychiatry" has done.

Kierkegaard. This school traces back to a Danish theologian and two German philosophers. The theologian, Soren Kirkegaard, was born in 1813 in Jutland and brought up in a time of evangelistic revival, when theology was talked about everywhere just as politics is now. He had much personal sorrow. In 1839 he wrote: "What the English say of their home, I have to say about my sadness, my sadness is my castle ... I am witty and people laugh, but I cry." In 1841 he broke an engagement and afterwards never married. His theology was opposed to the systematic theologians on the one hand and the mystics on the other. Both were one-sided and abstract, he said, avoiding involvement in the whole of life. He preached a theology of total commitment—whether to vocation, to marriage, or to faith. "Through having ventured to take a decisive step in the utmost intensity of subjective passion," he wrote, "and with full consciousness of one's eternal responsibility ... one learns something else about life, and learns that it is quite a different thing from being engaged, year in and year out, in piecing together a system. A true philosophy, articulating the intellectual, the aesthetic, and the ethical in the living body of an existing individual, would teach the inquirer to know and meet the requirements of his situation" (1).

The key phrase in these quotations is "an existing individual," in all his subjectivity and the emotional experience of his life. This emphasis upon individual existence, by Kirkegaard and his successors, led to the term "existentialist." Kirkegaard's intense subjectivism may have come from his own deep awareness of his sadness, dissuading him from cultivating the kind of abstract thought that ignored emotion and avoided involvement.

Husserl. It was the German philosopher Edmund Husserl who turned his attention to the inner experience of the individual, before any inferences were drawn as to its origins, or its objective meaning. He wished to look at this raw material of existence with fresh eyes. The natural scientist takes for granted the existence of an external world beyond the individual, which he experiences and interprets through his senses and his intelligence. Husserl urged the study of the subjective phenomenon itself— hence, he called his philosophy "phenomenology." In Ellenberger's words: "The observer ... excludes from his mind not only any judgment of value about the phenomena, but also any affirmation whatever concerning their cause and background; he even tries to exclude the distinction of subject and object and any affirmation about the existence of the object and of the observing subject" (2). Both Husserl and Freud, it is interesting to note, were students of Franz Brentano. Where Freud looked for the meaning behind his patient's words, Husserl looked at the inner experience itself, exactly as the subject described it.

Heidegger. Husserl's pupil, Martin Heidegger, is a German philosopher who has carried this mode of thought still further. Heidegger is very difficult to understand. His readers are inclined to find whatever they project into his works—a sort of verbal Rorschach. But certain concepts can be made fairly clear. He calls his philosophy "ontological" rather than existential—from the Greek word for "being" rather than the Latin one. He contrasts being in general with being as an individual—"Sein" with "Dasein," to use the German. "Dasein" means "being there" as a specific individual, born at one time and one place, within a social class or race, with his particular sex, intelligence, and other individual traits and capacities. Alfred North Whitehead, the late British philosopher, called each individual an "actual entity"—for we know life directly only through the actual experience of living people. Each of us, Heidegger says, is "thrown" or cast into life without being asked whether, where, or when he wanted to be born. This is the "human predicament," which we all share, with greater or less degree of awareness. Another important concept is that of "authenticity." In Heidegger's words' "authentic being [is] rooted in the explicit sense of my situation," while "inauthentic being [is] moving automatically in the established ruts and routes of the organized world;" as our young people might say nowadays, "going along with the system." Heidegger makes much of the awareness of death as the ultimate form of encounter with individual being. Death breaks all pretensions, without releasing us from responsibility in choosing and fulfilling the possibilities that are open to us while we are alive.

Jaspers. The first psychiatrist to make use of existentialist thought in understanding his patients was Karl Jaspers. After writing his text, *General*

Psychopathology, he became a philosopher. While Heidegger accommodated to the Nazi regime, Jaspers (though not a Jew) left Germany. Until after the second World War he was professor of philosophy at the University of Basel in Switzerland. He is now living in Germany again. In his textbook he describes the inner experience of many patients. He recognized that the patient, like the rest of us, cannot change his parents nor (ordinarily) his sex, nor his past, nor altogether the fate and fortune of his lot, but he can accept and adopt them and make them his own. This realization may be disillusioning and the source of despair, or it may be the beginning of self-transcendence. I am unique, but so is everyone else. My liberty assumes and requires the liberty of every other person, and also requires communication between each self, in order to establish authentic existence for all in the world.

Binswanger. The man who is most responsible for existential psychiatry is Ludwig Binswanger. There are many other existentialists who are literary men and theologians. Examples of literary men are the Frenchmen, Camus and Sartre. A theologian was Paul Tillich, another German, who left Nazi Germany and came to the United States and was professor of theology at Harvard. Still another theologian was Martin Buber, of Germany and Israel. Binswanger came from a celebrated family of Swiss psychiatrists. His father founded a mental hospital in Kreuzlingen on the Lake of Constance, and his uncle Otto was professor of psychiatry at the University of Jena in Germany. Ludwig first studied at Zurich under Eugen Bleuler and worked with Jung on the association test. He then studied psychoanalysis and became a fast friend of Freud's—the only one, it has been said, who remained a friend after disagreeing with the master over fundamentals. Before his death a few years ago he wrote a small and appreciative book of reminiscences of Freud (3).

Binswanger's title for his school of thought is *Daseinsanalyse*—the analysis of individual being. He sought out unusually articulate and self-perceptive patients with different psychiatric diagnoses, interviewed them exhaustively with infinite patience, trying to see and feel the patient's world with the greatest possible empathy. He wrote monographs on several patients, notably manics and schizophrenics, full of subtle clinical observations and philosophical interpretations based on Heidegger's work. They make hard reading, but are rewarding to the tenacious. Here, with Ellenberger's help(2), is an attempt at an interpretation.

With a little effort, most of us can understand each other because our worlds look pretty much alike. We take this correspondence for granted, not realizing that our common view of what is outside depends much upon the emotions we have projected into it because of our involvement.

When it comes to communicating and understanding perceptions and feelings about our bodies and our subjective reactions, difficulties multiply. A depressed patient or a schizophrenic whose libido has withdrawn from his environment, will have feelings of unreality (derealization), not because the world has changed, but because his attitude toward it is different. If his emotional involvement with his own body changes, then he will have depersonalization also. A depressed woman for example, said her limbs had changed to wood. A man with involutional melancholia even said that his body no longer existed. This ultimate degree of depersonalization is a kind of hypochondriacal delusion called "nihilism," and is more apt to involve just one organ, such as the stomach or the heart, than the whole body.

Binswanger, seeking to establish more general categories for understanding psychotic patients, discussed particularly changes in the perception of time and space. Subjective time is often different from time as measured by clocks. We all know how time passes much more quickly when we are busy and how slowly it goes when we are waiting or when we are bored. One of the main symptoms of depression is that time seems to pass with desperate slowness. Time stagnates—as though it had virtually stopped. A patient of Binswanger's refused to become old, dull, and ugly—in other words, she wanted to stop time. She lived as a "timeless ethereal wish-self." The future to her meant "unimpeded, unrestrained, ambitiously optimistic wishing, and yearning." While the depressive believes he has no future, and ruminates endlessly about the past, the manic lives in a limitlessly expanded future. A schizophrenic, on the other hand, may live in his own personal time more than in the world time, or he may lose all awareness of world time and live in an endless present.

Space also has its existential peculiarities. Binswanger speaks of the Umwelt, Mitwelt, and Eigenwelt—the "around-world," the "with-world," and the "own-world" (knowing German helps to understand existentialist psychiatry!). The first is environment as we naively perceive it—inanimate objects and situations, with their casual inhabitants. The second is the world of living beings to whom we relate emotionally and with whom we communicate. The last is the inner world of intuitions and feelings. The state of one world will determine our perceptions of the other two. Happiness expands space, sorrow constricts it, and despair makes it empty. To many an acute schizophrenic, the outer world is in danger of sudden catastrophic destruction. Perhaps it has already been destroyed, leaving him in utter isolation, alone with his "own-world." In mystical ecstatic experience space becomes "luminous," full of intense blinding light—so called "cosmic consciousness" (4). The mystic momentarily feels he has encompassed the whole of space and time within his own being—a foretaste of eternity. If overwhelmed by his visions he may not be able to return and becomes a chronic catatonic rather than a religious leader or a saint.

Storch. An existentialist psychiatrist who has paid particular attention to the phenomenology of schizophrenia is Alfred Storch, a great admirer of Ludwig Binswanger. One of his papers, entitled, *The question of existence among schizophrenics,* describes a catatonic case of the kind just mentioned, as follows (5):

A 31-year-old musician, with an unsuccessful father and a dominant but distant mother, discovered homosexual leanings in himself at puberty, arousing feelings of inferiority and isolation. Becoming attached to an out-going girl he wished to marry her, but she rejected him. His psychosis soon burst upon him in the form of acute catatonia. It began with a sensation of bright light, then a belief in his own extraordinary strength and immortality. This ecstatic state was followed by one of "decomposition," in which he believed that he was both living and dead, the last man living in a world which was changing and disappearing. He had made a pact with the Devil and God was dead. After insulin coma treatment and psychotherapy he was discharged from the hospital improved. Two years later he was still non-psychotic and more realistic.

While sane, according to Storch, the patient tried unsuccessfully to unite his divided personality. In his psychosis he expressed the extremes of existence. On the one hand was the world of light—the "Lichtwelt"— of complete fulfillment in eternity, beyond time, space and individual existence. On the other hand was the world of death, the abyss ("Abgrund") world, of hopeless-continual-returning-to-the beginning. In the one world past and future are annihilated, or else united in an eternal present. All futurity is immediately realized, in being and in knowledge. In the other, the past is eternal, the future unattainable—natural human progress and completion become impossible. One is spiritualization, illumination, initiation; the other, materialization, mortification, putrefaction. The illumination was not a state of bliss, such as mystics describe. It was tormenting, painful, like fire in his head—a consuming flame, arbitrarily conferred on him. In the psychosis each state alternated, or both were mixed in excruciating confusion.

Such formulations of the inner experiences of schizophrenics help us understand them and empathize with them. It is not surprising that schizophrenics resort to neologisms to try to tell us what they are going through. If we seem to appreciate what they are feeling we can better establish rapport and gain their confidence and their cooperation for our treatment, whether physiological, pharmacological, or psychotherapeutic. It requires great stretching of our own imaginations to comprehend, but it is well worth it in terms of our ability to help such lost and bewildered people.

Von Gebsattel. What do existential psychiatrists say about the non-psychotic psychiatric disorders? Von Gebsattel, a German, studied the inner world of the obsessive-compulsive neurotic (2). Such a patient is disturbed by things which appear to him to be ugly, dirty, repulsive, or disgusting. His world is devoid of friendly forms, or even of inoffensive and indifferent forms. All objects appear to be infected with decomposition and decay. The patient fights not so much against disgusting things as against a general background of disgust, a "counterworld" (opposed to the conventional world) of decaying forms and destroying powers. Von Gebsattel writes of the compulsive patient's "incapacity to let his energies stream into ... task-oriented self-development," underlying his overt symptoms, "a choking or blocking of the life course ... becoming is blocked and the past is fixated and orientation toward the future becomes impossible."

Boss. A Swiss, Dr. Medard Boss of Zurich, has written an existential analysis of sexual deviations (6). Boss studied psychoanalysis in Zurich, London, and Berlin, and analytical psychology with Jung, before being attracted to Heidegger's thinking. Sexual deviation, he wrote, is "one of the many possible concrete manifestations of certain states-of-being and world concepts ... destructive ... expressions of a disturbed dialectic between the mode-of-being of love and of being-in-the-world as an isolated, purposeful individual ..." Existence as an isolated, finite, rebelling being covered up the dual mode-of-being of love impenetrably and with excessive rigidity. Therefore, love enters only through peripheral apertures, or only after violent attempts at breaking through worldly limitations. Consequently patients can express their needs for love only through homosexuality, rape, or sado-masochistic practices. Boss also wrote an excellent book on the existential analysis of dreams (7), in which, contrary to Ludwig Binswanger's view, he asserted that the theory of an unconscious mind is unnecessary for the practice of existential psychiatry.

How can we apply some of the ideas of existentialist psychiatry to the understanding and treatment of our patients? Heidegger considers the awareness of death as the ultimate form of encounter with individual being. Full awareness of death bursts upon most of us only in adolescence. We can deny that death can touch us, through the "illusion of Invulnerability"—others may die, but not oneself—a not unusual belief of the young soldier. Adolescents may gamble with death, as though leaving fate to decide whether they live or die. So-called "Russian roulette" is the most striking example. An adolescent patient once said that he and

several friends were riding along a suburban road when the driver suddenly turned to the others and said, "Who wants to die?" Since no one objected he began speeding along the curving high-crowned road. Very soon the
car turned over. Several were injured but fortunately none died. Among
adolescent girls, suicide attempts of varying degrees of seriousness are the
favorite form of gambling with death.

In late adolescence and early adulthood each of us must either accept
the roles allotted to him or choose among alternative roles. Jaspers indicated what has to be accepted: one's sex, intelligence, health, station in
life, religion, and the inevitability of death. In rigid societies like traditional India, acceptance was expected. In a mobile, democratic society
like ours, many more choices are offered, with increasing anxiety and insecurity, as Erich Fromm has indicated. With us, we can choose, more or
less, regarding vocation, marriage, and religious faith. Each choice elimi-
nates other possibilities. Many young people find these decisions impossible or very difficult because they imply commitment. Some people go
on living a "provisional life," postponing important decisions indefinitely.
Many men and women have a succession of marriages and divorces, never
really committing themselves to marriage or to parenthood. The aim of
an authoritative religion, like old-fashioned Catholicism, is to expect commitment of its adherents: if once married, divorce is impossible, if once
pregnant, no abortion is allowed. The hope is that the absolute regulation
will force genuine involvement. If this hope is not realized, then emotional illness is a frequent result, with need for psychotherapy. Other possibilities are to leave the church, to remain a member in name only, or (as
is happening now) to change its practice from within. The same choices
have been forced upon fundamentalist Protestants and Orthodox Jews
for generations past.

Frankl. The middle-aged and aging exercise denial, postpone decisions,
avoid the inevitable, and put off death as long as possible. Victor Frankl,
who uses the term "logotherapy" for his existential approach, describes
(8) his getting a middle-aged woman to stop dressing like a teenager and
to accept her menopause. Compulsive personalities whose entire security
is invested in their jobs or in their roles as housewives, lose the essential
meaning of their lives when those roles can no longer be adequately filled.
So they resist retirement, cling to their children, and fail to develop other
reasons for living. Perhaps the recent rash of heart transplants is another
example of refusing to face the inevitable, on the part of the surgeons as
well as their patients. Loss of religious faith, and the failure to work out
a philosophical substitute, removes another underpinning (9).

Laing. Of those existential psychiatrists writing today, besides Medard Boss, and Victor Frankl, Ronald Laing is the best known. Ronald Laing is a brilliant Scotsman now practicing in London. His book, *The Divided Self* (10) is an excellent contribution to the phenomenological understanding of schizophrenia. He has not been content to work in a hospital, medical school, or in a private office, like most other psychiatrists. He has organized his own therapeutic community. Believing as he does that his patients are suffering from an invasion by the blind authority of our culture, he treats them without condescension. He considers himself, like Thomas Sczacz in this country, as the champion and protector of the mental patient, helping him in his attempts to preserve his individuality and to wake up himself and the world from the trance society tries to put its members into. As he says in *Politics of the Family:* "I consider many adults (including myself) are ... in a hypnotic trance ... Attempts to wake before our time are often punished, especially by those who love us most. Because they, bless them, are asleep. They think anyone who wakes up ... is going crazy. Anyone in this transitional state is likely to be confused. To indicate this confusion is a sign of illness, is a quick way to create psychosis" (11).

Existential psychiatry in this country has its own society, the American Ontoanalytic Association, and its own journal. Whether it will change the outlook of academic psychiatry as deeply as it would like to, will be seen in time.

BIBLIOGRAPHY

1. H. J. Blackham, *Six Existentialist Thinkers,* Routledge & Kegan Paul, London, 1962.

2. H. F. Ellenberger, in *Existence,* Basic Books, New York, 1958, p. 96-100:, V. E. VonGebsattel, "Existence," p. 170 ff.

3. L. Binswanger, *Sigmund Freud, Reminiscences of a Friendship,* Grune & Stratton, New York, 1957.

4. R. A. Clark: *Cosmic Consciousness in Catatonic Schizophrenia,* Psychoanalytic Review, 33, 460, 1946.

5. Alfred Storch, *Die Daseinfrage der Schizophrenen,* Schweitzer Archiv f. N. & P., 59, 330, 1947.

6. M. Boss, *The Meaning and Content of Sexual Perversions,* Grune & Stratton, New York, 1949.

7. M. Boss, *The Analysis of Dreams,* Philosophical Library, New York, 1958.

8. V. Frankl, *The Doctor and the Soul,* Knopf, New York, 1957.

9. V. Frankl, *Basic Concepts of Logotherapy,* J. Exist. Psychiat. 8, Spring 1962.

10. R. D. Laing, *The Divided Self,* Penguin Books, Baltimore.

11. R. D. Laing, *The Politics of Experience,* Pantheon, New York, 1967.

Chapter 10

THE SUMMING UP

When we think how many conflicting schools of psychiatry there are, we are apt to be confused and discouraged. How is it that psychiatrists, who are supposed to help others get along, can't get along with each other? If you add to the schools I have surveyed those additional ones formulated by psychologists, the question becomes even more relevant. Robert A. Harper in 1959 published a book, *Psychoanalysis and Psychotherapy: 36 Systems,* (1) the most exhaustive of several similar reviews.

A closer look should resolve some of this confusion and reduce our discouragement. Since the brain is the most complicated thing we know on earth—or perhaps in the whole universe, unless a higher evolved being is found on another planet—it is not surprising that its workings are hard to explain. Nor is it remarkable that several conflicting, even contradictory, theories will explain those workings equally well. We should not be too discouraged either, since so many theories and points of view are signs of creative activity and growth in psychiatry and psychotherapy. If controversy died down and new schools of thought and practice ceased to appear, we would be in a state of stagnation. If the doctrines of one school prevailed over all others, thinking would have crystallized into dogma.

This trend of thought suggests an analogy with religious denominations. Before the Reformation one system of theology prevailed throughout Christian Europe. All conflicting ideas were rigidly suppressed as heretical. With the ferment of the Renaissance, reformers arose in Germany, Bohemia, and Switzerland, challenging the authority of the universal Catholic Church. Within a century or two there were over 400 Protestant denominations in Europe and America, existing beside the Mother Church. R. A. Harper uses this analogy in describing the rebellion of the Neo-Freudians and others against the doctrines and practices of psychoanalysis: "The more rigid and fanatic of the Freudians react roughly in the fashion of religious fundamentalists. Tell a fundamentalist that you think many Biblical stories are ... allegories and myths, and he has had enough of you. Tell a fundamentalist Freudian that you question the efficiency of free association, the universality of the Oedipus Complex, or the three stages of infantile sexuality, and his reaction is much the same ... he knows your understanding of human behavior is superficial—(the Freudian equivalent of Satanic) ... Closed minds ... are equally evident in fanatics of other persuasions." Horney, Sullivan, "Adler and Jung (and those who orthodoxly follow these and other therapeutic Messiahs) show an unwillingness to listen objectively and to consider the possible merit of opposing positions." A friend of mine, Dr. Edward Humphreys, was accustomed to speak of the adherents of "Freudianity." When I was in Zurich I saw traces of "Jungianity" among those who were overcome by Jung's charisma.

Jung himself was well aware of the dangers of discipleship. One of my favorite quotations from his works goes as follows:

> "I would not deny ... the existence of genuine prophets, but I would begin by doubting each individual case. ... Every respectable prophet strives manfully against the unconscious pretensions of his role. ... But beside the possibility of becoming a prophet, there is another alluring joy ... the joy of becoming a prophet's disciple. ... The disciple is unworthy, modestly he sits at the Master's feet and guards against having ideas of his own. Mental laziness becomes a virtue: one can at least bask in the sun of a semi-divine being ... Naturally the disciples always stick together, not out of love, but for the ... purpose of effortlessly confirming their own conviction by engendering an air of collective agreement. ... One is a mere disciple, but nonetheless a joint guardian of the great treasure which the Master has raised ... deeming it a solemn duty and a moral necessity to revile others not of a like mind, to enroll proselytes and to hold up a light to mankind ... exactly as though one were the prophet oneself. ... Just as the prophet is a primordial image from the collective psyche, so the disciple ... is also a primordial image."(2)

A leader's followers, like the epigoni of Alexander the Great, are in themselves embodiments of an archetype figure. The greater the pioneer, the more difficult it is for those who come after to break away from his inspiration, do their own thinking, and go their own ways (3).

When Saul Rosenzweig, who devised the "Picture Frustration Study," was an undergraduate at Harvard he wrote an honors thesis on *The Psychology of Philosophers.* One could equally well write a study of the psychology of psychiatrists and psychotherapists. In fact, at the Northeast Community Mental Health Center in Philadelphia we have given the "Myers-Briggs Type Indicator" test, to determine our therapists' psychological types in accordance with Jung's classification. We can also then give the test to a selection of their patients to see what correlations we get, particularly in terms of correspondence or contrast between the types of therapists and patients, and the course and results of treatment. We cannot, unfortunately, get such objective data about the founders of the various schools, so we must resort to speculation. Jung supposed that Freud and Adler disagreed because Freud's attitude-orientation was extraverted, while Adler's was introverted. Even more extraverted, to my mind, would be the attitudes of organically oriented clinical psychiatrists and behavior therapists. Dr. Joseph Wolpe, in fact, disparages the benefits of subjectively-oriented psychotherapy entirely. I have called this "devaluation of the psyche," as though he and other behaviorists have a resistance against introspection, or perhaps, an incapacity and consequent distaste for it. Clinical psychiatrists of neuro-psychiatric bent are happy to make diagnoses, prescribe medication, give electro-shock, or appear in court—fortunately for us psychotherapists who (in our introverted way) find such activities tiresome. Jung hemself, in his autobiography (4), describes the interaction throughout his life between his extraverted and introverted sides. In later years he became more introverted, as his writings reflect. Certainly, existentialist psychiatrists like Ludwig Binswanger show deep introversion in their preoccupation with their patients' subjective experience. In terms of Jung's "functional types," one may classify the classical Freudians with their love of theory, and the existentialist with their delight in abstractions and fine distinctions, as "thinking types"—the one extraverted, the other introverted. Among intuitives we could consider Stekel extraverted and Jung introverted. Ferenczi, with his concern about emotions, and perhaps Rank also, emphasizing relationships as he did, may be thought of as "feeling types," while Wilhelm Reich, who idealized the orgasm, had perhaps introverted sensation most highly developed. When you think of your colleagues you can readily see that some are more active and some more passive. I recall a child psychiatrist of whom it was said that if non-directive therapy hadn't been thought of he would have invented it, he was so quiet and passive in personality.

We can, therefore, say that not only do pioneers originate forms of theory and practice appropriate to their personalities, but students and youthful therapists often pick that school which most suits them. As with religion, one's beliefs and behavior are influenced by the doctrine one is originally taught. The rebels from their training, of whichever school, are those whose temperaments take to a different approach than that favored by their professors. A young therapist who wants quick results, who prefers action, and is not particularly interested in theory (in other words, an extraverted inuitive) will take up some form of "reality therapy," involving "group activity," "encounters" or "confrontation," or "transactional analysis." Analytic treatment, Freudian, Jungian, Rankian, or otherwise, appeals to the theoretically-minded introvert who is more fomfortable in a two-person relationship. It is a bit amusing to see adherents of different schools insisting on the rightness of their doctrines and methods, when what they mean is that what they think and do is right for them, because of their temperaments. In their turn patients tend to seek out that therapist who is best suited to their needs—not only for understanding or empathy, but also perhaps for passivity or manipulation. Whoever assigns cases in a Mental Hospital or Health Center, should keep these needs, both therapists' and patients,' well in mind.

Another distinguishing feature among schools of psychiatry is whether or not they resort to a "reductive" approach to their material and their theories. It was characteristic of both Freud and Adler, at least in their earlier periods, to reduce their observations to one primary drive and to derive everything else from that drive. In Freud's work, the primary drive was of course the sexual instinct or *libido*. "Aggression" resulted from sexual jealousy and fear, while "civilized behavior" arose through sublimation of sexuality. Adler reversed the formula, by making aggression primary, an expression of the "power drive." "Sexual conflict" came from competition between the sexes, and "civilization" arose through the intelligent recognition of "social interest," resolving competition between individuals.

Jung, as described in Chapter 8, sought to synthesize these contradictory views by supposing both the sexual and aggressive drives to be derived from undifferentiated "psychic energy." We shared with the rest of animal creation the capacity for direct ex-expression of these drives. Only the human race was capable of direct formation, through "archetypal images," of *culture* and *civilization,* transform-

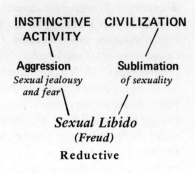

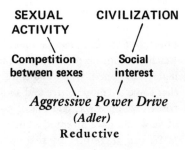

Figure 1.

ing the world about us by *projection* and creative activity. Otto Rank [as interpreted by Progoff (5)] put forward similar conceptions. What Jung called "psychic energy," Rank called the "will." Where Freud and Jung conceived of the will as that portion of libido, or psychic energy available for the service of the ego, Rank considered the will to be primary, underlying all conscious and unconscious activity, corresponding perhaps to the Jungian "Self." Rank derived sexual, and aggressive, and artistic energy from this primary source.

A true synthesis of all the observations and theories so far presented awaits another genius of the caliber of Freud and Jung. A Danish psychiatrist, Jarl Wagner Smitt, some years ago spoke of the need of a general psychological theory common to psychiatry, psychology, and the

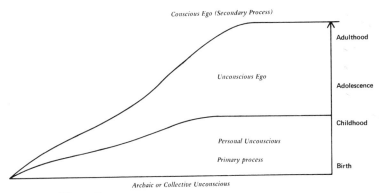

Figure 2. DEVELOPMENT OF THE LEVELS OF THE PSYCHE

social sciences (6). In fact, a recent personal communication from him says that he has such a theory nearly ready for publication, intending to account for infantile autism, schizophrenia, and manic-depressive psychosis in terms of hormonal breakdowns at three crucial stages of learning. I shall venture some tentative formulations in a diagrammatic way— always recognizing that diagrams, however valuable as teaching aids, are gross over-simplifications of the complexity of the human mind. The first diagram is one I used in a paper published in 1961 comparing Freudian and Jungian dream theory (7). The development of the *ego* and of *secondary process thinking* is represented by the line rising above the *primary process* base. They grow further apart throughout childhood and adolescence, into adulthood. In the normal person, the *secondary process perception and thought* is ordinarily interrupted by primary material only during sleep. Through dreams the conscious personality may become aware of unconscious images and needs from all three levels—the unconscious ego, the personal unconscious and the archaic or collective unconscious. Some dreams emphasize one level, other dreams another. Complete interpretation should take all into account. Where a dream gives advance notice of physical illness even the organic level, underlying the other three, may be brought into awareness. Any or all these levels may also break through into consciousness during the course of neurotic or psychotic illness, or by way of creative or religious experience.

Another way of showing the levels of the psyche graphically is by a "layer cake" diagram, Fig. 3. If we arrange the levels one on top of the

CULTURAL MILIEU	FROMM, SOCIAL PSYCHIATRY
SOCIAL RELATIONSHIPS	RADO, HORNEY
FAMILY RELATIONS	FREUD, SULLIVAN, RANK
EGO	ADLER, BEHAVIORISM, EXISTENTIAL, ANNA FREUD
PERSONAL UNCONSCIOUS	FREUD, KLEIN, SZONDI
ARCHAIC, COLLECTIVE UNCONSCIOUS	JUNG
PHYSICAL ORGANISM	ORGANICISTS

Figure 3.

other, from the physical organism to the cultural milieu, the social and family relationships will represent group ties above the ego. On the lower side of the ego are the two unconscious levels, personal and collective, shading off into the organic through the psychophysiologic. The different schools each have applied themselves to one or more levels, with a good deal of overlapping. When considering one level the theories and observations appropriate to that level are applied. So a place for each is found, avoiding much controversy over whether one theory is "true" or not. All together they give a comprehensive explanation of the whole gamut of human experience. For example, when concerned with a sex deviate,

Freud's theories may be entirely adequate for understanding and treatment. If confronted with an acute schizophrenic with Messianic delusions, Jung's ideas may be more useful.

Of all other disciples who broke with Freud the one for whom it was most difficult was Otto Rank. Freud set Rank's feet upon his career while still a university student. For 20 years, especially when he was a member of the "ring," they were most closely associated. But Rank's own creative urge had to assert itself and finally forced him to separate. He thus illustrated in himself his own theory of separation-anxiety arising with the birth of a new stage of ego development, recapitulate—the birth trauma.

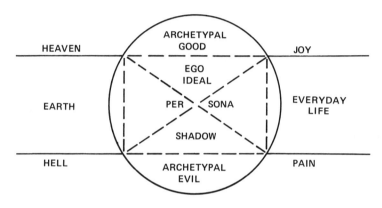

Figure 4.

Like Jung, Rank sought for ways to transcend individual existence, finding a meaning for life, beyond everyday living and beyond death. He called it the "search for immortality." This search had already been described by Plato in his dialogue, the *Symposium.* Freud's patients often avoided the existential anxiety of individualization by remaining absorbed in family relationships. Adler and Fromm advocated identification with the welfare of society. Jung recognized the religious solution either by way of a traditional church or through mystical religious experience. Rank, like Plato, saw that the artist found an identity in his own creative productions, whether literature, music, painting, or otherwise, while alive. After death he lived through their persistence, as well as during the life of his own reputation. As Horney would say, they searched for glory—real or illusory. In Jung's terms, they also embodied the hero archetype, in the form of artistic fame. Momentarily in the creative act artists participated in eternity, just as the ordinary man or woman does in sexual climax or the religious man does during a ceremony or in midst of mystical ecstacy.

I have summarized all this in another diagram, Fig. 4. A theologian,

Bishop Robinson of the Church of England, said in a book, *Honest to God*, popular a few years ago, that in New Testament times the universe was portrayed in three levels. Above was Heaven, below was Hell, and in between Earthly Life. The purpose of life was to live our earthly existence in such a way that we would escape Hell and gain Heaven. The religious life gave believers a foretaste of heaven and the timeless existence of eternity, during the time they struggled with vicissitudes of the middle realm. Modern man, said Robinson, could no longer believe in this three-level universe, because "Heaven" was now only outer space, and "Hell" molten iron in the earth's core. My contribution is to suppose that the New Testament cosmogony was a projection by the people of that time into the universe of their own experience. Prosaic every-day living, with its routine of work and family life, was the middle level, pain and sorrow were "Hell on earth," while intoxication and religious life were "Heaven." Modern man, skeptical about religious doctrine, or wishing to avoid pain, sorrow, and boredom, searches for "supernatural" experience while still alive, rather than deferring "bliss" until after death.

On the left side of the diagram we see the New Testament levels, Heaven, Earth, and Hell, and on the right the modern experiences of joy, everyday life, and sorrow. In the center is a square within a circle, representing (very roughly) the life of an individual. The "square" stands for those phlegmatic folk who are content with the tepid pleasures of the workaday world. They adapt to the world with their *personas,* their *ego ideals* and *shadow repressions.* Those who become emotionally ill, or who are creative personalities or who are not content with an average life, suffer or seek intrusions from the worlds above or below them. If they are sick they will expand into the manic elated experience, or contract down into the depressive world, or, like Storch's catatonic, they will be torn between both. Drug-users deliberately seek the upper level through amphetamines, hallucinogens, or opiates. They may find themselves, however, thrown into the lower world when they "crash" or have a "bad trip" or undergo withdrawal symptoms. The question therapists should ask is, how can we learn to strengthen defenses against such intrusions, to tolerate reasonable amounts of stress and anxiety, and to enjoy life, whether by medications or psychotherapy or by social, artistic, or religious means? For the drug user the alternative is, how can he "turn on" without drugs?

If we are going to help our patients, more than we do, prevent more illness and raise the level of mental health we need all the ideas we can get. We can't afford to overlook the contributions of any school of thought. We need to encourage physiological and pharmacological research, to sharpen our psychotherapeutic skills, and keep our minds open for new insights. The founder of a school is like a miner who taps a new lode. His followers work it till the lode peters out, in a generation or two. Further progress depends upon the discovery of a new vein. As far as prevention goes, we need to spend as much time and skill and money on learning how to raise children and foster harmonious family life as we do on furthering careers and making money. We need to know a lot more about "social psychiatry," namely, the relationships between poverty and racial problems and mental illness, and the psychopathology of demogogy and international relations.

As a final word, what can I say to each of you as individuals? First, don't be rigid and orthodox about anything. On the contrary, keep your mind open for new ideas, from others and from within yourself, always against a background of historical perspective. Second, find the theoretical outlook and the method of practice that is congenial to your own temperament, learn all you can about it and put them to work with all the enthusiasm and involvement you've got. And don't be scornful or superior about what others are sincerely trying to do. On these principles you can't go far wrong and will end helping many troubled people.

*

BIBLIOGRAPHY

1. R. A. Harper, *Psychoanalysis and Psychotherapy, 36 Systems*, Prentice Hall, Englewood Cliffs, N. J. 1959.

2. C. G. Jung, *Two Essays on Analytical Psychology, Collected Works*, Vol. 7, Pantheon, New York, 1953.

3. R. A. Clark, M.D., *Analytic Psychology Today*, Am. J. Psychotherapy, 15, 193, 1961.

4. C. G. Jung, *Memories, Dreams, Reflections*, ed. by A. Jaffe, Pantheon, New York, 1961.

5. Ira Progoff, *The Death & Rebirth of Psychology*, Julian Press, New York, 1956.

6. Jarl Wagner Smitt, *Need of a General Psychological Theory Common to Neuro-Psychiatry, Psychology and the Social Sciences*, Acta Psychiatrica et Neurologica, 23, 10, 1948.

7. R. A. Clark, *Jungian & Freudian Approach to Dreams*, American J. of Psychotherapy, 15, 89, 1961.

8. J. A. Robinson, *Honest to God*, Westminster Press, Phila., 1963.

INDEX